Lesson Plan a la Carte™

Integrated Planning for Students
With Special Needs

Valerie Paradiz, PhD
Todd Germain, OTR, LCSW
Sarah Olivieri, MPS
Michelle DeFelice Haverly, MS

P.O. Box 23173
Shawnee Mission, Kansas 66283-0173
www.aapcpublishing.net

PUBLISHING

P.O. Box 23173
Shawnee Mission, Kansas 66283-0173
www.aapcpublishing.net

Publisher's Cataloging-in-Publication

Lesson plan a la carte : integrated planning for students with special needs / Valerie Paradiz ... [et al.]. -- Shawnee Mission, Kan. : AAPC Publishing, c2012.

p. ; cm. + CD-ROM.

ISBN: 978-1-934575-92-5
LCCN: 2011939180
Includes bibliographical references.
Summary: System teams can ensure consistency and thoroughness in lesson plans and learning objectives for students with special needs. Forms and blank templates are available on accompanying CD-ROM.

1. Teachers of children with disabilities--Handbooks, manuals, etc. 2. Autistic youth--Education--Study and teaching. 3. Autism spectrum disorders--Treatment. 4. Autism--Treatment. 5. Asperger's syndrome--Patients--Treatment. I. Paradiz, Valerie, 1963-

LC4717.8 L47 2012
371.94--dc23 1111

This book is designed in ITC Stone Sans and American Typewriter.

Printed in the United States of America.

CONTENTS

INTRODUCTION

The purpose of this book is to make your life as a school professional more structured, more effective, and easier when it comes to supporting students with special needs. Our team worked hard for several years to develop a lesson-planning model with you in mind. Whether you're a teacher, an administrator, or a clinician – and whether you're planning alone or in a team – *Lesson Plan a la Carte* can be an indispensable tool for supporting students with individualized education programs (IEP) and 504 plans. We know you have limited time in your busy schedule to prepare for lessons. This protocol will help you make the most of what little planning time you do have to …

- modify existing lesson plans
- create new lesson plans
- author a specialized curriculum
- prep for a self-contained special education setting
- plan for integrating a student with special needs into your general education classroom (alone or with a co-teacher or para)
- prep solo for your class
- plan collaboratively with a team

Lesson Plan a la Carte not only helps you teach a well-designed lesson, it also guides you through a step-by-step process of creating an *integrated plan*, bringing together learning objectives *and* therapeutic supports your students need directly in your classroom. Moreover, the model provides your school or education agency with practical protocols for organizing and documenting modifications, specially designed instruction (SDI), and response to intervention (RTI), helping you to truly walk the talk of data-driven decision-making (DDD) as it is mandated in the reauthorized IDEA (2004). As this slim volume indicates, we don't want to add more to your plate; we want to make it simpler to manage.

What Is Integrated Lesson Planning?

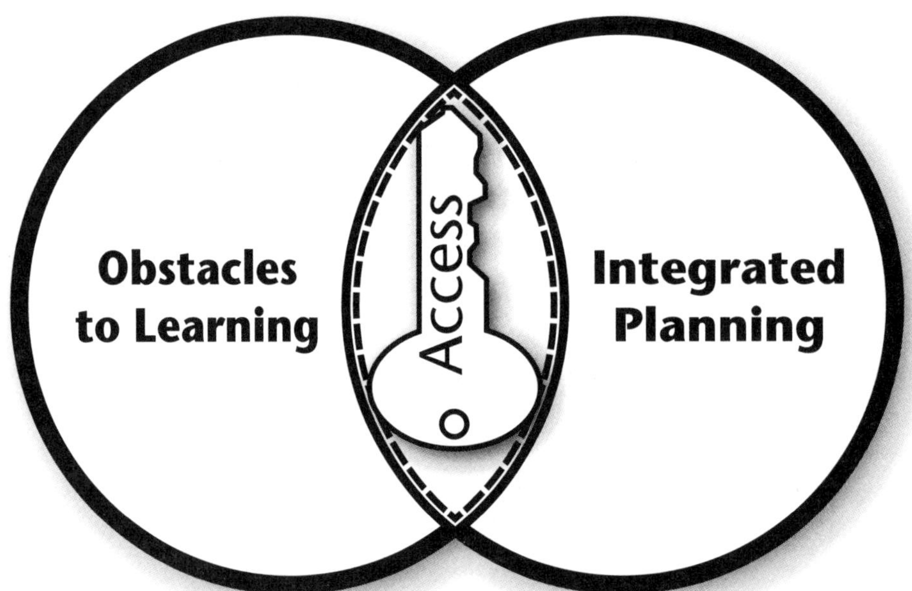

Integrated planning helps you overcome obstacles and provide access to learning.

If men are from Mars and women are from Venus, as the title of the famous self-help book by John Gray says, you might use the same words to describe teachers and clinicians. These two species often think, speak, and work differently in schools, and they often have divergent priorities and goals. *Lesson Plan a la Carte* integrates best clinical and educational practices into a plan that speaks a common language and aligns and focuses priorities, goals, and strategies.

Multiple worlds exist within the educational universe. Integrated planning happens when each of these worlds (teaching, clinical, administrative, etc.) has ready access to the perspectives and methods of the other, and most important, when all of the planning is directed toward one goal: removing students' *obstacles to learning* and replacing them with *access to learning*.

The *a la Carte* Concept and Its Authors

We called this book *Lesson Plan a la Carte* because we want you to think of it as a menu of possibilities. When you go into a restaurant and order a meal *a la carte*, you pick and choose from the menu whatever suits your particular tastes and needs. This is the fundamental concept of this lesson-planning model. As you use it, working alone or collaboratively with a team, you are guided through a system of menus that help you understand and pinpoint the particular needs of a student or a group of students. Then, following a template for writing a lesson plan or modifying one you already have, presto, you're ready to implement!

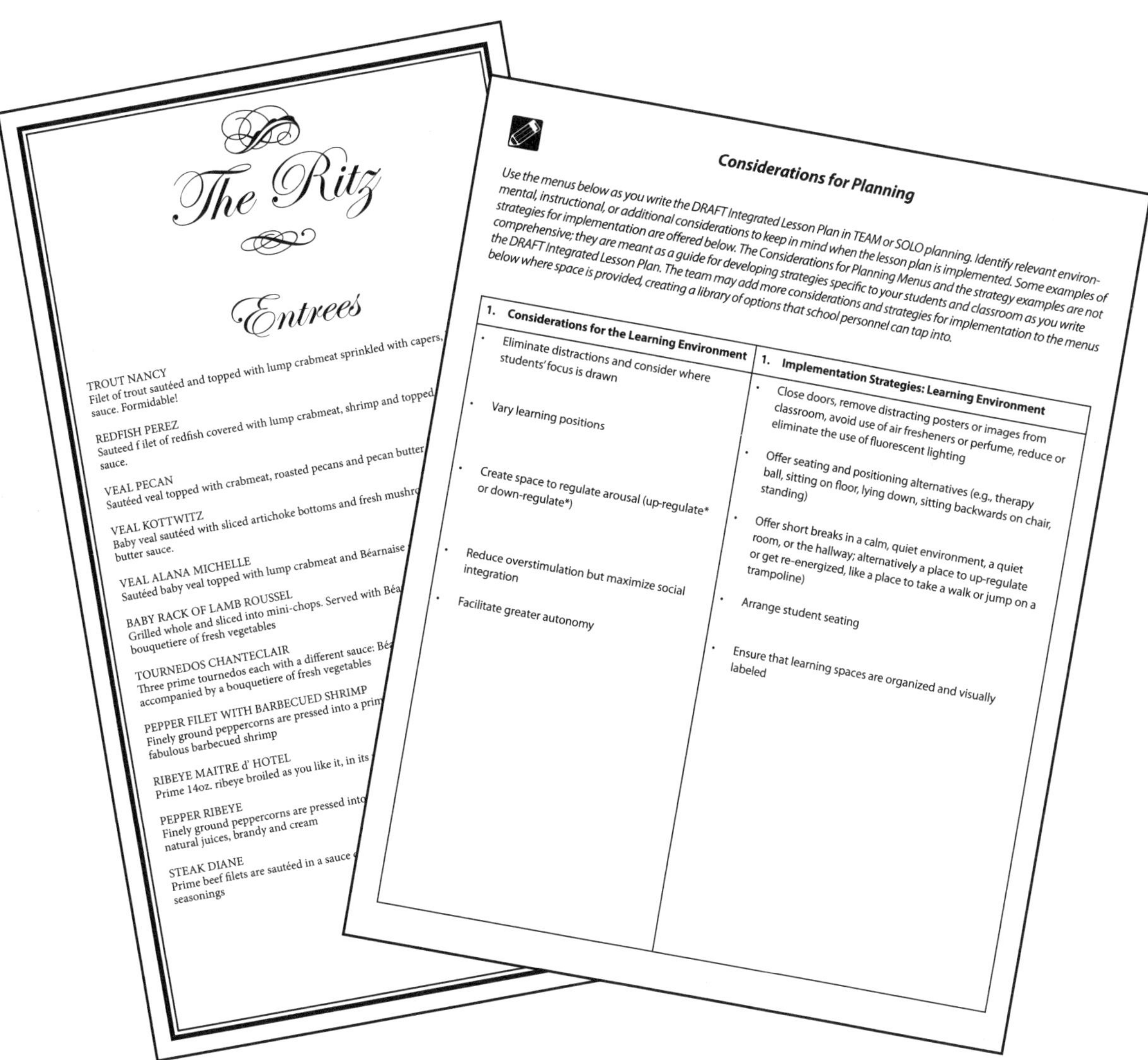

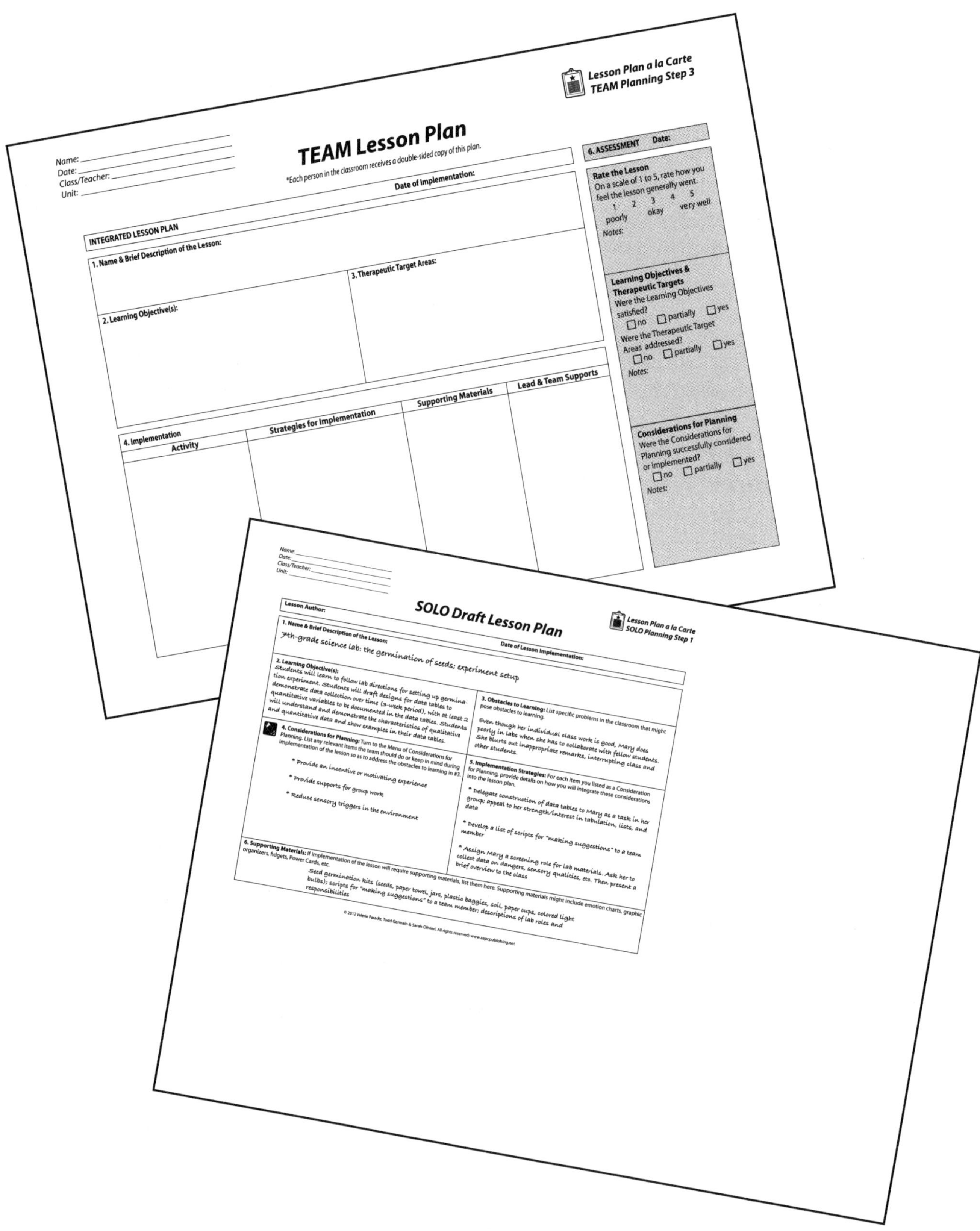

Lesson Plan a la Carte
TEAM Planning Step 3

Name:
Date:
Class/Teacher:
Unit:

TEAM Lesson Plan

*Each person in the classroom receives a double-sided copy of this plan.

Date of Implementation:

INTEGRATED LESSON PLAN

1. Name & Brief Description of the Lesson:

2. Learning Objective(s):

3. Therapeutic Target Areas:

4. Implementation Activity	Strategies for Implementation	Supporting Materials	Lead & Team Supports

6. ASSESSMENT Date:

Rate the Lesson
On a scale of 1 to 5, rate how you feel the lesson generally went.
1 2 3 4 5
poorly okay very well
Notes:

Learning Objectives & Therapeutic Targets
Were the Learning Objectives satisfied?
☐ no ☐ partially ☐ yes
Were the Therapeutic Target Areas addressed?
☐ no ☐ partially ☐ yes
Notes:

Considerations for Planning
Were the Considerations for Planning successfully considered or implemented?
☐ no ☐ partially ☐ yes
Notes:

Name:
Date:
Class/Teacher:
Unit:

Lesson Author:

SOLO Draft Lesson Plan

Lesson Plan a la Carte
SOLO Planning Step 1

1. Name & Brief Description of the Lesson:
7th-grade science lab: the germination of seeds; experiment setup

Date of Lesson Implementation:

2. Learning Objective(s):
Students will learn to follow lab directions for setting up germination experiment. Students will draft designs for data tables to demonstrate data collection over time (3-week period), with at least 2 quantitative variables to be documented in the data tables. Students will understand and demonstrate the characteristics of qualitative and quantitative data and show examples in their data tables.

3. Obstacles to Learning: List specific problems in the classroom that might pose obstacles to learning.
Even though her individual class work is good, Mary does poorly in labs when she has to collaborate with fellow students. She blurts out inappropriate remarks, interrupting class and other students.

4. Considerations for Planning: Turn to the Menu of Considerations for Planning. List any relevant items the team should do or keep in mind during implementation of the lesson so as to address the obstacles to learning in #3.
* Provide an incentive or motivating experience
* Provide supports for group work
* Reduce sensory triggers in the environment

5. Implementation Strategies: For each item you listed as a Consideration for Planning, provide details on how you will integrate these considerations into the lesson plan.
* Delegate construction of data tables to Mary as a task in her group; appeal to her strength/interest in tabulation, lists, and data
* Develop a list of scripts for "making suggestions" to a team member
* Assign Mary a screening role for lab materials. Ask her to collect data on dangers, sensory qualities, etc. Then present a brief overview to the class

6. Supporting Materials: If implementation of the lesson will require supporting materials, list them here. Supporting materials might include emotion charts, graphic organizers, fidgets, Power Cards, etc.
Seed germination kits (seeds, paper towel, jars, plastic baggies, soil, paper cups, colored light bulbs); scripts for "making suggestions" to a team member; descriptions of lab roles and responsibilities

While founding a school for middle and high school students with Asperger Syndrome and related conditions, Valerie Paradiz (co-author of this book) witnessed what seemed to be a recurring problem: Although many students were capable of learning and reaching specific academic goals, a variety of obstacles to learning prevented or slowed their progress, sometimes unnecessarily closing doors to important avenues for further learning and success. In response, Dr. Paradiz devised a menu-based model with the vision of finding a straightforward method for educators to integrate learning objectives with therapeutic supports and necessary modifications right in the classroom, and to be able to do so whether they were working alone (e.g., as a solo teacher in a general education classroom) or as a team (e.g., as a case study group, a co-taught class, or in teacher/clinician collaborations). Her goal was to address social, environmental, and communication challenges that block kids' access to academics and other learning.

The result of these efforts, *Lesson Plan a la Carte,* has since been successfully piloted in a variety of private and public, self-contained and integrated, classroom settings under the guidance of all the co-authors. Sarah Olivieri, a specialist in humanistic multicultural education, helped develop the model with a focus on benefiting *all* students in a classroom, whether they have an IEP or a 504 plan or not. She is also the ace designer of all the tools and menus you'll soon be putting to use. Todd Germain, who has worked as both an occupational therapist (OT) and a clinical social worker in schools and private practice, provided the clinical underpinnings for this book. One of his chief aims was to help families and schools avoid the pitfalls of squandering precious resources by providing alternatives to extensive (and often expensive) outside testing and support services. In Todd's experience, this approach to supporting students outside the school environment rarely translates into plans that involve and benefit children directly in their school.

In practice, *Lesson Plan a la Carte* has proven itself in a variety of settings. Jessica Lally, director of curriculum at LearningSpring School of New York City, describes how the model has influenced her organization, an elementary and middle school for students with autism spectrum conditions:

> *When you walk into a classroom where the Lesson Plan a la Carte model is being used, you see and feel the difference compared to a classroom where it's not present. Staff know just what to do and when. Instructional adaptations for one or more students are crystal clear and implemented in a way that naturally blends academic learning with therapeutic support.*[1]

Schools and programs such as LearningSpring, the Cooke Center for Learning and Development,[2] and the Open Center for Autism[3] have implemented *Lesson Plan a la Carte* systemically in their programs for development of original curricula, as well as modification of pre-existing and state-mandated curricula. As you learn to use this model, you'll have many opportunities to read tips and testimonials from staff schools and programs like these, who have actively used the *a la Carte* tool each day with efficiency and success.

---

1 Jessica Lally, MA, director of curriculum, LearningSpring School, New York, New York, in an interview on August 6, 2010 (www.learningspringschool.org).

2 The Cooke Center for Learning and Development is comprised of a network of elementary, middle, and high schools (K to age 21) for students with a broad range of developmental disabilities. It is the largest provider of inclusion services in New York City (http://www.cookecenter.org/).

3 A non-profit organization in upstate New York formerly directed by Sarah Olivieri, the Open Center for Autism offered a variety of after-school and camp program options for students with autism spectrum conditions by developing original curriculum using the Lesson Plan a la Carte system.

Common Challenges for Educators

Teachers, clinicians, and administrators are being asked more frequently than ever before to respond to students with an increasingly complex set of needs and behaviors. You are asked to address sensory, motor, language, and communication issues, as well as manage the social-emotional needs of students, all while trying to differentiate learning and meet curriculum mandates. Add to this the demands of documenting intervention fidelity (through RTI or other protocols), and you might find yourself in over your head. Take, for example, a school counselor who is leading a social skills group. In this instance, intervention fidelity would have to extend to the classroom as well, where the teacher must plan his lessons in a way that integrates the counselor's goals, objectives, strategies, and methods with his own learning objectives. Expectations such as these increasingly present greater demands on educators.

Professional Isolation

Over the years, research has shown that traditional "push-in" and "pull-out" interventions alone are insufficient to address the obstacles to learning and complex needs of students in today's school environment.[4] Pull-out methods take students out of other important curricular activities, require kids to generalize learning across contexts, and create a disorganizing effect on classroom schedules and small-group instruction. Push-in services can also create dynamics that are difficult to resolve. The following is an excerpt from a consultation with a teacher and a clinician working in a self-contained science class that may ring a bell with you.

Over the years, research has shown that traditional "push-in" and "pull-out" interventions alone are insufficient to address the obstacles to learning and complex needs of students in today's school environment.

> *Ms. Johnson, a speech-language therapist, teaches a push-in lesson for Ms. Aaron's ninth grade science class. Ms. Johnson establishes a Language Concept of the Week lesson that Ms. Aaron, in the beginning, is enthusiastic about, thinking that her students might benefit from a closer examination of the meaning of abstract concepts in her curriculum.*
>
> *One day in class, the speech therapist presents a lesson on the term* to observe, *a concept she feels should be appropriately understood in a science class. However, the classroom teacher is confused. In her mind, the timing of the Language Concept of the Week is all off, since student observations of scientific results or experimental effects in a lab aren't central to her learning objectives at this point in the unit. The result: The science teacher is left with the feeling that the push-in speech service "takes away precious lesson time." In response, Ms. Aaron decides to ask Ms. Johnson to present a lesson on the concept and use of rubrics, since the class will be using rubrics in the upcoming week to organize data. However, the speech therapist feels this is not an appropriate therapeutic role for her. "Teaching rubrics," she says, "is neither my area of expertise nor something I'd feel comfortable doing."*

4 Case-Smith, J., & Holland, T. (2009). Making decisions about service delivery in early childhood programs. *Language, Speech, and Hearing Services in Schools, 40*, 416-423.
Murawski, W. W. (2010). *Collaborative teaching in elementary schools: Making the co-teaching marriage work!* Thousand Oaks, CA: Corwin.

Clearly, this is a case of neither of the two professionals finding a way to integrate her objectives in a lesson, with the result that each feels being "put upon" and misunderstood. Indeed, many professionals in schools find themselves isolated from the very colleagues who could be useful to them in problem-solving classroom challenges, due to the training and experience that creates the Venus and Mars worlds we spoke of earlier.[5]

Reports of a different type of professional isolation come from general education teachers who express feeling overwhelmed by the demands of integrating a student with special needs into their classrooms with limited or no access to clinicians and without adequate professional development.

> *Mr. Shore, a high school biology teacher, has a student named Mary in his ninth-grade general education class. While Mary is very bright and gets a nearly perfect score on all her assignments and tests, she is very disruptive in the classroom, blurting out inappropriate remarks, particularly during labs or group work ("Someone stinks in here." "Turn off that light. It hurts my eyes!").*
>
> *When Mr. Shore speaks with Mary about her behavior, she seems to understand that her remarks in class are inappropriate and that they distract Mr. Shore and others from the current activity. Mary apologizes and promises not to do it again, but she still cannot seem to stop herself. Mr. Shore has run out of ways to get through to Mary. When she interrupts, he asks her to leave the room and go to the counselor's office. He is fed up with having her in his class.*

Here is a case of a general education teacher who does not have access to simple OT strategies that he could implement easily and directly in the classroom. Additionally, Mr. Shore doesn't have time in his busy day to seek out the school district's OT, whose schedule is limited on his campus. In fact, he may not even know that Mary's challenges are sensory-based because he hasn't had the professional development training necessary to inform him about how sensitivities to light, or even smell, can become obstacles to learning for many students with special needs.

Limited Time for Lesson Planning and Documentation

Another significant challenge that educators must deal with daily is the limited amount of time we have to prep for class, and do it well. Let's face it, as educators supporting children with IEPs or 504 plans, we find ourselves so busy tracking goals, modifications, and related services to be sure we're fulfilling state and federal requirements that clerical demands sometimes seem to consume our day. In all honesty, having to use up our precious planning time to be sure we're crossing every bureaucratic "t" and dotting every red-tape "i" sometimes seems to impede our ability to genuinely support our students.

Finally, even if we do have the necessary planning time, we often have no protocol in place for creating the kind of *integrated lesson plans* we dream of: Lessons that are individualized for a student, a particular group of students, or an entire classroom and that address obstacles to learning in real time right in the classroom. What we teach is important, but HOW we teach it is all the more important. If we are

---

5 To peek ahead and see a fully developed integrated lesson plan for a science class using the Lesson Plan a la Carte model, see pages 52-53.

to fulfill federal mandates for data-driven decision-making regarding a student's ongoing progress and educational plan, we need a real method for it – one that we can rely on, that helps us fuse learning objectives with therapeutic supports and accommodations, that addresses professional isolation in our schools (whether we are planning as teams or alone!), that produces consistent documentation of the complex learning activities we design, and that ultimately validates the way we aspire to teach each day we show up for work. This is where *Lesson Plan a la Carte* comes in.

> *"When I use this planning method, it doesn't mean I have extra busy work. It's the kind of classroom tool you have and you use, and it serves your documentation purposes."*
>
> Michelle DeFelice Haverly, MS, Special Educator, NYSUT Trainer and Content Developer

The Telephone Game

Remember the telephone game? You probably played it as a child. First one child whispers a short sentence into another child's ear. That child then turns and whispers it to another child. That first utterance gets passed from one person to another the same way, but by the time the message has passed through a dozen people, it has become so different from the original that it has everyone giggling hysterically. You're probably thinking, "Oh yeah, I remember that game. But what does it have to do with lesson planning?"

This game illustrates the humor of human communication when it breaks down, but it also demonstrates the negative effects of isolation. There is no way in this game to enrich one's understanding through feedback from others, no spirit of interdependence by which members of the group support and are empowered by each of the other members. As far-fetched as it might seem, it's not a stretch to imagine a similar scenario in a school.

For example, imagine an incident involving a student with a pattern of disruptive talking. Another student tells a para-educator about it, who in turn tells the lead classroom teacher. Attempting to follow the instructions of a counselor, the teacher asks the teaching assistant to talk to the student about respecting the personal space of others. When the teaching assistant intervenes with the student, the student indignantly calls out, "I didn't do that!"

What the teaching assistant in this scenario doesn't know is that this student has difficulty with self-monitoring and reading social cues, and so he doesn't see his own behavior as disruptive. What the counselor doesn't know is that this behavior tends to happen during math and science. What the teacher doesn't catch is that the behavior tends to occur when the student has finished his work far ahead of the other students. The intervention, which ends up sounding something like, "stop bothering your classmates," is a far cry from what the counselor might have intended. This is because there hasn't been an opportunity to bridge professional perspectives and share strategies within the educational team.

Further, while we strive to foster the capacity for independence, and ideally interdependence, among our students, that goal may only be realized to the degree that interdependence has been achieved among ourselves as educational team members.

Now that our teams are using Lesson Plan a la Carte *regularly, everybody agrees that it really does help organize their thoughts and their planning. It points us in a better direction before we even begin to implement a lesson.*

Jessica Lally, MA, Director of Curriculum, LearningSpring School, New York City

Put differently for those who don't plan in teams but are working solo in their classrooms or clinical offices: If we don't have easy avenues of accessing perspectives other than our own, we might be playing the worst kind of telephone game of all – with only one player. That's a lot of pressure for solo planners. Or worse, maybe we don't even know how alone we are because we have no input or feedback from other professional perspectives ... many general education teachers find themselves in this situation every day.

The Fork in the Road: Two Possible Scenarios

One of the first and most vital steps in integrated lesson planning is to engage in structured sharing of professional perspectives. Whether you are creating/modifying lesson plans and curriculum alone or with a team, *Lesson Plan a la Carte* helps bridge the gaps discussed above and bring multiple perspectives into play as you develop a lesson. All it takes is a little shift in how you approach your planning, and some simple protocols to assist you with that. Consider the team planning example below, keeping in mind that if you are planning solo, without team support, your time will come, so please read on!

> *Paul is a seventh grader with ASD in a general education classroom. He has been sent to the office for disciplinary actions several times for "correcting the teacher" and being "generally rude." Paul is given an in-school suspension, and a school counselor devises a behavior plan that reinforces positive behaviors and provides for consequences for negative behaviors. Paul tries hard, and for a while the number of referrals to the office for him diminish.*

Based on this example, one could say that the intervention was effective from a behavioral perspective – one might even assert that this is what really matters. But what has Paul really learned? Have his needs really been met? Or are there underlying issues still standing as obstacles to his learning in the classroom? However, there are two issues that we need to take a look at. What has the teacher learned about the counselor's take on this child? And what has the teacher learned about responding to the social-emotional needs of students in general? What has the counselor learned about how this teacher understands this student in the context of the classroom and students' behavior in general? How have these two professionals grown and enriched each other through this encounter? Now, let's rewind and see the difference.

> *Paul is a seventh grader with ASD in a general education classroom. He has been sent to the office for disciplinary actions several times for "correcting the teacher" and being "generally rude." A team consisting of the teacher, counselor, and speech-language therapist creates a series of lesson plans that integrate the counselor's sense of Paul as having difficulties with perspective taking, the speech-language therapist's understanding of Paul's pragmatic language difficulties, and the teacher's sense that Paul is socially isolated in the classroom and struggles in large-group formats. As a result of this team planning, the teacher puts an emphasis on small-group instruction, clarifies and highlights Paul's role among his peers, and makes explicit expectations of his behavior during the lessons using language he understands.*

Aside from the question of efficacy, the point here is that this teacher has learned a great deal about perspective-taking and pragmatic language skills, and the clinicians have learned about the social dynamics and language demands of this classroom, not to mention how teachers view and respond to those dynamics. These professionals can now apply what they have learned in future encounters with similar students and related issues. Not only is their sense of isolation and professional stagnation reduced, they have also built a foundation for a proactive system that addresses academic, social-emotional, and behavioral obstacles to learning.

Benefits of *Lesson Plan a la Carte*

In summary, there are some significant challenges when it comes to planning integrated lessons for students with special needs. *Lesson Plan a la Carte* is here to help make the process clear and efficient for you or your team while addressing common challenges observed in classrooms. In the upcoming pages of this manual, we'll provide you with

- An introduction to key concepts in integrated lesson planning
- A clear, step-by-step planning protocol that's efficient and effective
- Guided worksheets for writing original integrated lesson plans or curricula
- Guided worksheets for modifying existing lesson plans to make them more integrated
- Methods for identifying a student's, group of students', or classroom's particular obstacles to learning
- Inventories of strategies to support your lesson-planning process, with the goal of providing students access to learning
- Protocols for conducting purposeful, organized team meetings

- Templates for documenting and substantiating instructional practices
- Follow-up lesson plan assessments that include both qualitative and quantitative data collection
- Additional assessment options for your internal or state-level documenting and reporting needs
- Opportunity to build a library of integrated lesson plans for your greater school community

As you proceed to the next chapters of this book, you will learn key concepts to get you thinking about, and perhaps redirect, your approach to lesson planning. Then, we'll provide you with the hands-on tools you need to get started creating integrated lesson plans![6]

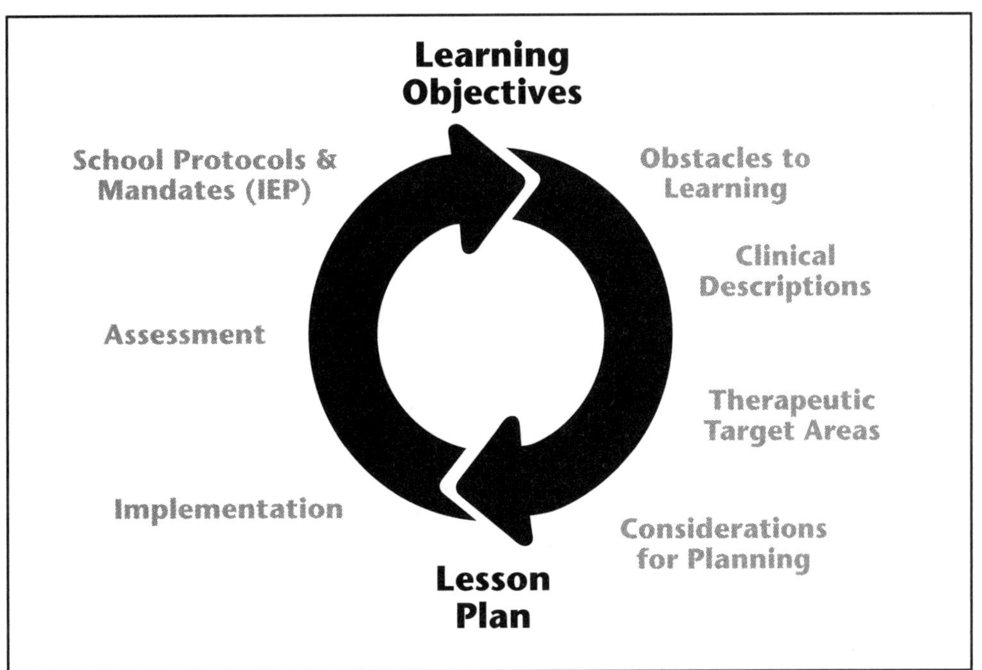

The Steps of the Lesson Plan a la Carte Process

6 *The Ziggurat Model Release 2.0* (Aspy & Grossman, 2012) and the *Comprehensive Autism Planning System (CAPS)* (Henry & Myles, 2007) are complementary resources that address these same challenges from different points of departure (not strictly lesson planning) (see Appendix A).

CHAPTER 1

THE INTEGRATED PLANNING PROCESS: CONCEPTS AND FOUNDATION

No doubt you have written your fair share of lesson plans in your educational career, and if we were to survey lesson plans drawn from a variety of sources and settings, they would contain many similar elements. As our team developed this manual, we had a particular purpose in mind: to examine the steps that a single teacher or a team of educators move through as they plan an intervention or lesson and then teach it. Using these observations, we created *Lesson Plan a la Carte*, piloting it as a lesson-writing tool in a variety of schools. The result is a protocol that keeps you on track in not only getting the plan written, but in creating an *integrated lesson*.

In the following pages, you will read through the key concepts of the *Lesson Plan a la Carte* planning process. While many of the planning stages will be very familiar to you, you will note that the emphasis is on combining your current learning objectives with the supports and modifications your students need, whether they are drawn from the functional behavioral assessment/behavior intervention plan (FBA/BIP) process or IEP accommodations and goals – or simply out of necessity because there are challenges you need to address right now for a student or group of students.

For example, teaching a student how to interact appropriately with others in small-group situations might not seem to be your responsibility as an eighth-grade English/language arts (ELA) teacher. You might even think, "That's something for the social skills therapist to take care of." And yet, what if addressing a particular student or group of students' need for this support in real time, right in your classroom, would immediately reduce paralyzing interruptions so the entire class could work well? What if, in doing so, you just aided a student, and by extension his social skills counselor, in generalizing a skill he never understood how to bring out of a self-contained social group session into the real world? What if this process were so inherently linked to the academic content you were teaching that you were satisfied with having covered your own curricular demands? The *Lesson Plan a la Carte* method will ask you to consider such options by providing you with small cues and pointers through each phase of planning a lesson.

Learning Objectives

*Quite often, the behavioral issues we see are **access to learning** issues in disguise. However, extinguishing behaviors shouldn't be our objective; removing **obstacles to learning** is our primary goal. Simple observation, with support from the **therapeutic menus**, can lead us to identifying a variety of **underlying causes** for the obstacles to learning our students face: sensory/regulatory, social/emotional, language/communication and organizational.*

We asked high school teachers and clinicians from a self-contained special education classroom to respond to the following question: Is your program a therapeutic school with academic curriculum or an educational program with therapeutic elements? The teachers almost unanimously replied that it was a therapeutic school, and the clinicians claimed it was primarily an educational program. As it turns out, each group felt their objectives for students were secondary to those of the other. We find it vital to keep this point clear: **Learning objectives are always the focus in educational settings. Behavior is not an objective. It is an outcome.**

Learning objectives can vary in scope and focus, depending upon short-term goals (e.g., "Students will summarize the plot of a chapter in a novel.") or upon externally determined goals that you are expected to achieve (e.g., providing mandated curriculum to students or covering specific state standards or units of a textbook that your school has purchased for you to teach). Other types of learning objectives don't involve academic content but might address life skills (e.g., "Students will learn how to dial 911 in emergency situations."). Additionally, objectives might involve one student or an entire group or class. Sometimes, you might even find yourself in situations where the learning objectives or curriculum aren't predetermined and you have to establish your own (for example, when creating a new specialized program with a team in your school). **Whatever the case may be, knowing the learning objective(s) is the essential first step in writing a lesson plan.**

Obstacles to Learning

What if a student with special needs in a high school chemistry class always blurts out the answers to questions before others have a chance to raise their hands? What if a girl in a middle school ELA class gets up and walks out of the room, unannounced, without ever indicating her intentions or needs?

Obstacles to learning often appear as behavioral issues, such as "zoning out," "shutting down," or as group dynamics that can undermine or even paralyze an entire learning period (e.g., a student who gets "wound up" whenever he's assigned to work with a partner or small group).[7]

7 Many students do not inherently know how to get ready to learn. They don't know how to regulate themselves so that they can profit from instruction. Thus, it is important that this obstacle to learning be bridged prior to adult-led lessons. For example, Judy Endow's book *Practical Solutions for Stabilizing Students with Classic Autism to Be Ready to Learn: Getting to Go* (2010) provides information on how to accomplish this goal.

A recent study of middle and high school students in general and special education settings, published in the *Journal of Positive Behavior Interventions*, links unaddressed behavioral challenges directly to academic performance and risk of failure.[8] Likewise, *Disability Scoop* reporter Shaun Heasley writes that "the high rate of discipline among special education students is often the result of built-up frustration on the part of educators who simply don't know what to do with kids who present challenging behaviors."[9] Heasley's report is based on recent records from the Texas Department of Education that indicate "for every 100 students with disabilities there were nearly 56 in-school suspensions and 25 out-of-school suspensions in one academic year." By comparison, "numbers for typically developing students hovered around 33 in-school suspensions and 12 out-of-school suspensions."[10]

You can't carry around all your students' IEPs while you're teaching a lesson. This planning model helps you consolidate that information and even makes it easier to address multiple needs of multiple students in one setting.

Michelle DeFelice Haverly, MS, Special Educator, NYSUT Trainer and Content Developer

Quite often, the behavioral issues we see are **access to learning** issues in disguise. As we mentioned in the discussion of learning objectives above, extinguishing behaviors shouldn't be our learning objective; removing obstacles to learning, on the other hand, is our primary goal in writing an integrated lesson plan. Often, simple observation can lead us to identifying a variety of obstacles our students face, and, if you think about it, we frequently already know what those obstacles will be well before we even teach a lesson. It doesn't matter if we don't know the reason for the obstacles we see, **just naming them is an important step in moving closer to understanding the underlying causes and in ultimately achieving the primary goal, the learning objective**.

Clinical Descriptions and Therapeutic Targets

What is the reason for, and value of, a clinical perspective in the lesson plan? Speech-language, OT, PT (occupational and physical therapy), and counseling perspectives help us begin to interpret the obstacles to learning we observe. When we are able to identify possible underlying causes for these obstacles, such as sensory issues, we move deeper, almost by design, into integrated planning. At this moment, **we begin to look at the *whole* student in her learning environment.** We appreciate how classroom demands and dynamics, as well as learning expectations, are brought to bear on the student's ability to learn when she has sensory, cognitive, communication, regulatory, or other differences. These are the "aha" moments in planning that bring us closer to our students. **We become attuned to *how* to provide the access they need to learn well.** Defining one or more therapeutic targets to be addressed within the lesson plan can help us even further by focusing our efforts and attention to a specific need or modification.

8 McIntosh, K. et al. (2008, October). Relationships between academics and problem behavior in the transition from middle school to high school. *Journal of Positive Behavior Interventions*, 10(4), 243-255.

9 Shaun Heasley, *Disability Scoop*, August 16, 2010, www.disabilityscoop.com

10 Shaun Heasley, *Disability Scoop*, August 16, 2010, www.disabilityscoop.com

Considerations for Planning

When we have identified obstacles to learning and decide to address them by combining best teaching and therapeutic practices, we are faced with the reality of "How am I actually going to do this?" This is another critical juncture in the integrated lesson planning process. It is where we must depart from clinical theory and consider how to move what we have discovered about a student or group of students into practice.

Special considerations for planning emerge here. We might need to modify how an assignment is taught or make adjustments in the environment. We might need to bring about a shift in the group dynamics in a particular class or change the way communication between students or between the teacher and the students happens. Strategies emerge and are integrated into the lesson plan.

Modifications generated by the a la Carte planning process, while implemented for one specific student with special needs, can also benefit other "typical" students in the general education classroom. In fact, sometimes I can combine all integrated students' needs into one lesson plan, with the help of a la Carte. Other times I use it to write a lesson plan for a single student. Ultimately, the final lesson plan gives proof and documentation that I have implemented the modifications and accommodations of the IEP.

Michelle DeFelice Haverly, MS, Special Educator, NYSUT Trainer and Content Developer

The Lesson Plan

The integrated lesson plan is the written culmination of all of the concepts we have described thus far. It is anticipatory in that it has not yet been put into action. Yet you (if working alone) or your team have considered the learning objectives, identified the obstacles to learning, and, as a result, have created a plan that combines this information and knowledge into something you think can effectively be put into practice during implementation. The goal: to successfully address social, emotional, environmental, communication, and other challenges that block students' access to academics and other learning, while still making good on your own teaching demands.

Implementation

There are two key elements in successfully implementing an integrated lesson plan.

The first key is **preparation**. Through the *a la Carte* planning process, you will design a carefully crafted and well-organized lesson plan. A key part of this process is writing down **how the lesson will be implemented in the classroom**. This written plan is essential for making sure that the lesson includes the various therapeutic components that it needs and that all of the professionals in the classroom know what their role is.

The second key to successfully implementing an integrated lesson plan is to **follow through**; that is, you must carry out the plan with fidelity. This sounds simple, but in the reality of the classroom, it takes focus and self-discipline. The authors of this book have seen well-respected educators – in the middle of a hard and chaotic day – throw all of their training, knowledge, and preparation out the window when stress got the better of them. Having a written plan in hand, and providing copies of it to each of the educators in the room before implementation, can be your best ally during those tough days when chaos reigns.

My biggest advice for educators who use this model would be to make sure to use the assessment tool that's included. It's really helpful in making you sit down and think about your lesson for five minutes in order to figure out what could be done next.

Jessica Lally, MA, Director of Curriculum, LearningSpring School, New York City

Assessment

Assessment of how implementation of a lesson went can happen in a variety of ways and can have as its focus a variety of targets, ranging from student outcomes, to classroom or programmatic outcomes, to self-assessment of your teaching. If you recall for a moment just how much you are asked as an educator to address the complex needs of your students, all the while trying to differentiate learning and meet curriculum mandates, you will understand how critical taking the time for assessment is. Whether to document curricular modifications, specially designed instruction (SDI), response to intervention (RTI) or any other data requirements, assessment in the *a la Carte* system provides you with the protocols, structures, and flexibility you need to empower yourself in practicing data-driven decision-making (DDD).

Finally, assessment brings you full circle to where you first began in the lesson planning process. And while it can be useful for a variety of clerical reasons or for fulfilling internal, IEP, or state-level reporting requirements, what it ultimately does is *validate* the hard work you do each day you show up for your students.

CHAPTER 2

GETTING TO KNOW THE MENUS

Now that you are familiar with the integrated lesson planning process, let's take a closer look at the hands-on tools you'll be using to guide you. Take a look again at the flow chart here to refresh your memory on the steps you'll move through as you plan.

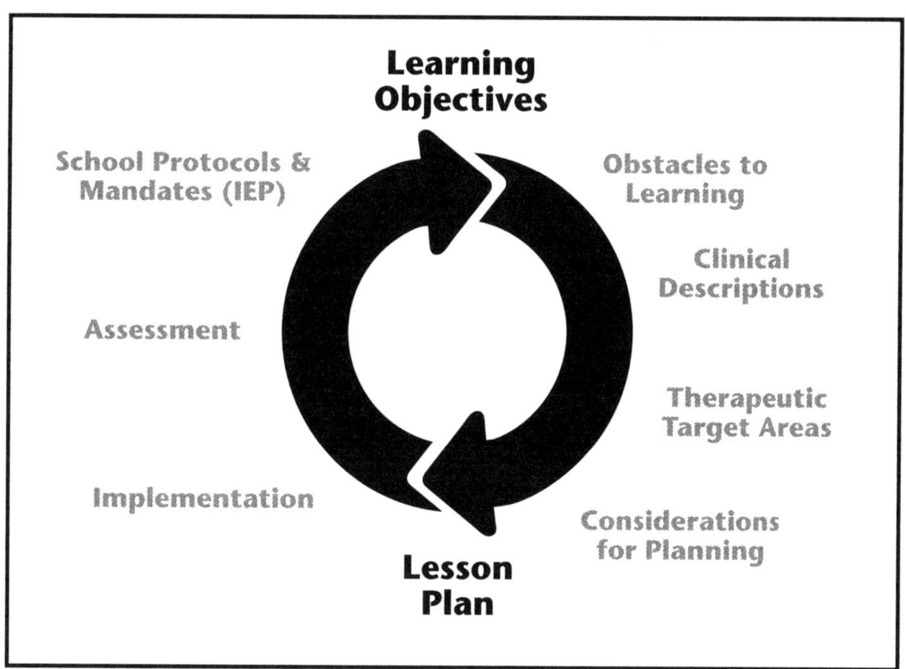

The Menus

The core components of the *Lesson Plan a la Carte* planning model are its menus. You will become familiar with them quickly when you begin to write your own lesson plans, but for now, it's helpful to know that there are two types of menus, which are identified throughout this manual with special icons for easy use:

Considerations for Planning Menus

These menu sets will support you in the lesson planning and writing process. You will turn to them often. In fact, you'll read through them each time you create a new lesson, picking and choosing items the same way you would if you were ordering *a la carte* from a menu in a restaurant.

Using the Therapeutic Menus

When you have identified the particular obstacles to learning of a student, or a group of students, it's helpful to "translate" those obstacles into a format that gives you a basis for deciding which therapeutic areas to target within the lesson plan. While not exhaustive, we have grouped the areas in which students typically experience challenges into four categories, each represented by menus:

1. Language & Communication Menu
2. Attention & Executive Functioning Menu
3. Social & Emotional Menu
4. Sensory & Regulatory Menu

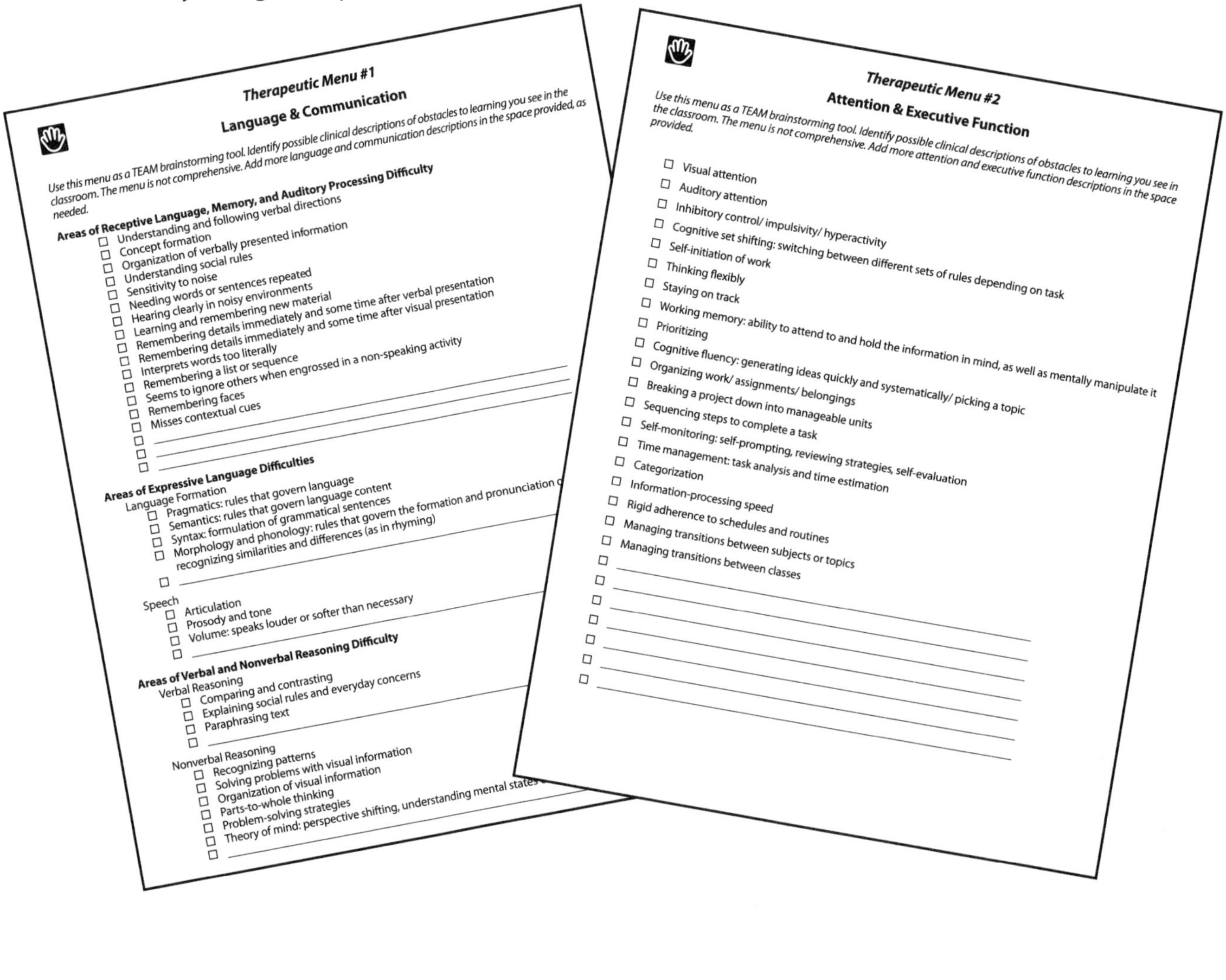

Therapeutic Menu #1

Language & Communication

Use this menu as a TEAM brainstorming tool. Identify possible clinical descriptions of obstacles to learning you see in the classroom. The menu is not comprehensive. Add more language and communication descriptions in the space provided, as needed.

Areas of Receptive Language, Memory, and Auditory Processing Difficulty

- ☐ Understanding and following verbal directions
- ☐ Concept formation
- ☐ Organization of verbally presented information
- ☐ Understanding social rules
- ☐ Sensitivity to noise
- ☐ Needing words or sentences repeated
- ☐ Hearing clearly in noisy environments
- ☐ Learning and remembering new material
- ☐ Remembering details immediately and some time after verbal presentation
- ☐ Remembering details immediately and some time after visual presentation
- ☐ Interprets words too literally
- ☐ Remembering a list or sequence
- ☐ Seems to ignore others when engrossed in a non-speaking activity
- ☐ Remembering faces
- ☐ Misses contextual cues
- ☐ ____
- ☐ ____
- ☐ ____

Areas of Expressive Language Difficulties

Language Formation

- ☐ Pragmatics: rules that govern language
- ☐ Semantics: rules that govern language content
- ☐ Syntax: formulation of grammatical sentences
- ☐ Morphology and phonology: rules that govern the formation and pronunciation [illegible] recognizing similarities and differences (as in rhyming)
- ☐ ____

Speech

- ☐ Articulation
- ☐ Prosody and tone
- ☐ Volume: speaks louder or softer than necessary
- ☐ ____

Areas of Verbal and Nonverbal Reasoning Difficulty

Verbal Reasoning

- ☐ Comparing and contrasting
- ☐ Explaining social rules and everyday concerns
- ☐ Paraphrasing text
- ☐ ____

Nonverbal Reasoning

- ☐ Recognizing patterns
- ☐ Solving problems with visual information
- ☐ Organization of visual information
- ☐ Parts-to-whole thinking
- ☐ Problem-solving strategies
- ☐ Theory of mind: perspective shifting, understanding mental states
- ☐ ____

Therapeutic Menu #2

Attention & Executive Function

Use this menu as a TEAM brainstorming tool. Identify possible clinical descriptions of obstacles to learning you see in the classroom. The menu is not comprehensive. Add more attention and executive function descriptions in the space provided.

- ☐ Visual attention
- ☐ Auditory attention
- ☐ Inhibitory control/ impulsivity/ hyperactivity
- ☐ Cognitive set shifting: switching between different sets of rules depending on task
- ☐ Self-initiation of work
- ☐ Thinking flexibly
- ☐ Staying on track
- ☐ Working memory: ability to attend to and hold the information in mind, as well as mentally manipulate it
- ☐ Prioritizing
- ☐ Cognitive fluency: generating ideas quickly and systematically/ picking a topic
- ☐ Organizing work/ assignments/ belongings
- ☐ Breaking a project down into manageable units
- ☐ Sequencing steps to complete a task
- ☐ Self-monitoring: self-prompting, reviewing strategies, self-evaluation
- ☐ Time management: task analysis and time estimation
- ☐ Categorization
- ☐ Information-processing speed
- ☐ Rigid adherence to schedules and routines
- ☐ Managing transitions between subjects or topics
- ☐ Managing transitions between classes
- ☐ ____
- ☐ ____
- ☐ ____
- ☐ ____
- ☐ ____
- ☐ ____
- ☐ ____

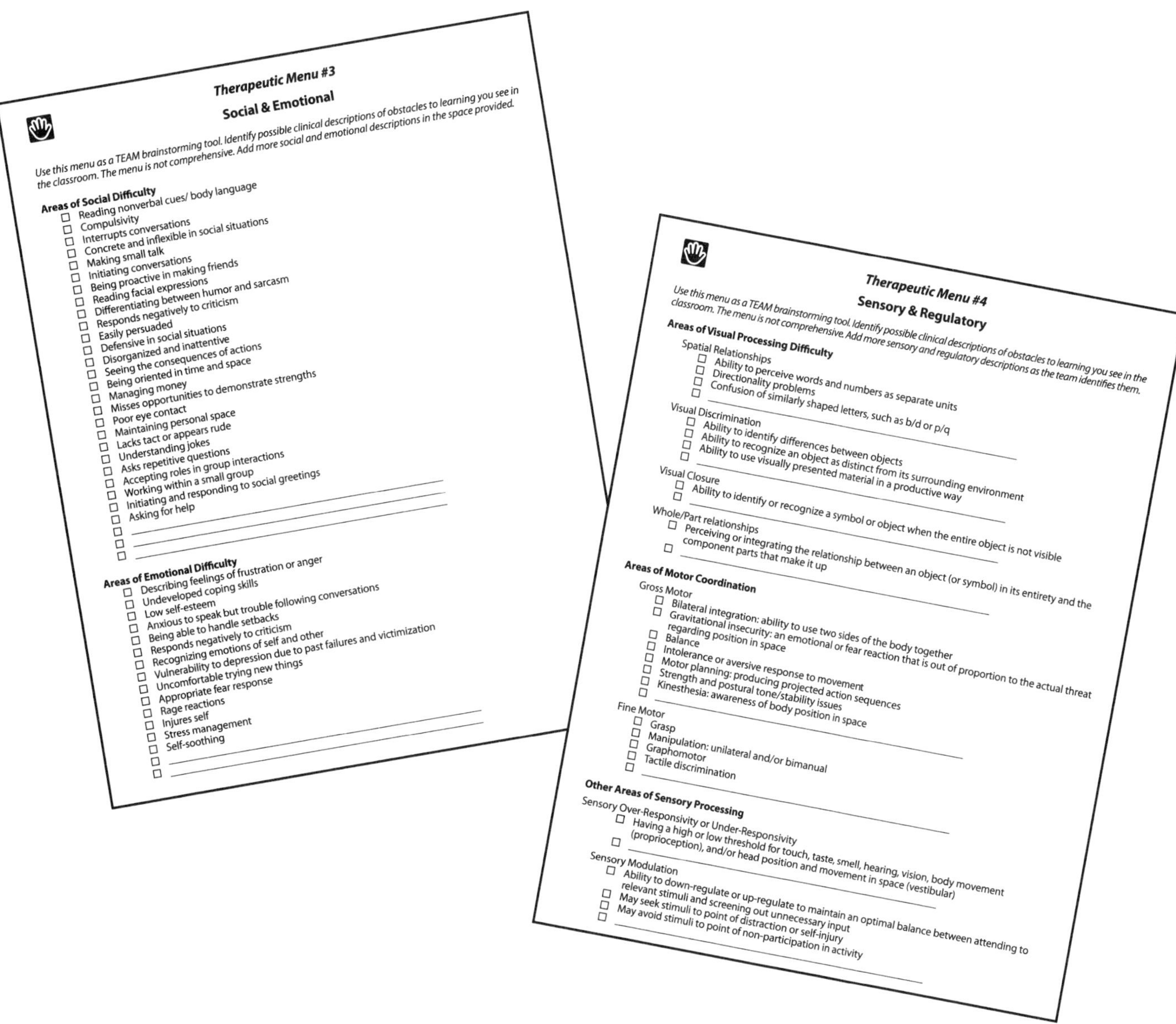

Therapeutic Menu #3

Social & Emotional

Use this menu as a TEAM brainstorming tool. Identify possible clinical descriptions of obstacles to learning you see in the classroom. The menu is not comprehensive. Add more social and emotional descriptions in the space provided.

Areas of Social Difficulty

- ☐ Reading nonverbal cues/ body language
- ☐ Compulsivity
- ☐ Interrupts conversations
- ☐ Concrete and inflexible in social situations
- ☐ Making small talk
- ☐ Initiating conversations
- ☐ Being proactive in making friends
- ☐ Reading facial expressions
- ☐ Differentiating between humor and sarcasm
- ☐ Responds negatively to criticism
- ☐ Easily persuaded
- ☐ Defensive in social situations
- ☐ Disorganized and inattentive
- ☐ Seeing the consequences of actions
- ☐ Being oriented in time and space
- ☐ Managing money
- ☐ Misses opportunities to demonstrate strengths
- ☐ Poor eye contact
- ☐ Maintaining personal space
- ☐ Lacks tact or appears rude
- ☐ Understanding jokes
- ☐ Asks repetitive questions
- ☐ Accepting roles in group interactions
- ☐ Working within a small group
- ☐ Initiating and responding to social greetings
- ☐ Asking for help
- ☐ __________
- ☐ __________
- ☐ __________

Areas of Emotional Difficulty

- ☐ Describing feelings of frustration or anger
- ☐ Undeveloped coping skills
- ☐ Low self-esteem
- ☐ Anxious to speak but trouble following conversations
- ☐ Being able to handle setbacks
- ☐ Responds negatively to criticism
- ☐ Recognizing emotions of self and other
- ☐ Vulnerability to depression due to past failures and victimization
- ☐ Uncomfortable trying new things
- ☐ Appropriate fear response
- ☐ Rage reactions
- ☐ Injures self
- ☐ Stress management
- ☐ Self-soothing
- ☐ __________
- ☐ __________

Therapeutic Menu #4

Sensory & Regulatory

Use this menu as a TEAM brainstorming tool. Identify possible clinical descriptions of obstacles to learning you see in the classroom. The menu is not comprehensive. Add more sensory and regulatory descriptions as the team identifies them.

Areas of Visual Processing Difficulty

Spatial Relationships
- ☐ Ability to perceive words and numbers as separate units
- ☐ Directionality problems
- ☐ Confusion of similarly shaped letters, such as b/d or p/q
- ☐ __________

Visual Discrimination
- ☐ Ability to identify differences between objects
- ☐ Ability to recognize an object as distinct from its surrounding environment
- ☐ Ability to use visually presented material in a productive way
- ☐ __________

Visual Closure
- ☐ Ability to identify or recognize a symbol or object when the entire object is not visible
- ☐ __________

Whole/Part relationships
- ☐ Perceiving or integrating the relationship between an object (or symbol) in its entirety and the component parts that make it up
- ☐ __________

Areas of Motor Coordination

Gross Motor
- ☐ Bilateral integration: ability to use two sides of the body together
- ☐ Gravitational insecurity: an emotional or fear reaction that is out of proportion to the actual threat regarding position in space
- ☐ Balance
- ☐ Intolerance or aversive response to movement
- ☐ Motor planning: producing projected action sequences
- ☐ Strength and postural tone/stability issues
- ☐ Kinesthesia: awareness of body position in space
- ☐ __________

Fine Motor
- ☐ Grasp
- ☐ Manipulation: unilateral and/or bimanual
- ☐ Graphomotor
- ☐ Tactile discrimination
- ☐ __________

Other Areas of Sensory Processing

Sensory Over-Responsivity or Under-Responsivity
- ☐ Having a high or low threshold for touch, taste, smell, hearing, vision, body movement (proprioception), and/or head position and movement in space (vestibular)
- ☐ __________

Sensory Modulation
- ☐ Ability to down-regulate or up-regulate to maintain an optimal balance between attending to relevant stimuli and screening out unnecessary input
- ☐ May seek stimuli to point of distraction or self-injury
- ☐ May avoid stimuli to point of non-participation in activity
- ☐ __________

As illustrated, each of these menus consists of lists of possible clinical descriptions (or underlying causes) for the obstacles to learning that you or your team are observing. Note that they are not meant to diagnose a student or suggest a definitive causal relationship between an obstacle to learning and a specific deficit. Behavioral, academic, and social difficulties in the classroom may have underlying causes in multiple categories or even in multiple areas within a particular menu. As you'll see, the Therapeutic Menus are used primarily as a brainstorming tool, before you even begin to design or write a lesson plan. Thus, the point of their use isn't to find the "right" item on the menu. Similarly, in the brainstorming stage, there aren't any "wrong" descriptions. Instead, you're simply perusing the menu, seeking any variety of ways to describe the issues you've identified as obstacles to learning. (To see the complete Therapeutic Menus, turn to page 64 of the Appendix or refer to the CD included with this book.)

Now let's take a moment to look at samples of each of the four types of Therapeutic Menus and do some exercises so you can familiarize yourself with them.

Language & Communication Menu

As you can see in the sample menu below, we have broken down the Language & Communication Menu items into three major areas where students commonly show challenges:

1. Receptive capacities
2. Expressive capacities
3. Verbal and nonverbal reasoning abilities

Below we've listed some common obstacles to learning educators encounter in their classrooms. Using the sample Language & Communication Menu provided to the right, try your hand at choosing clinical descriptions that might best explain the underlying cause.

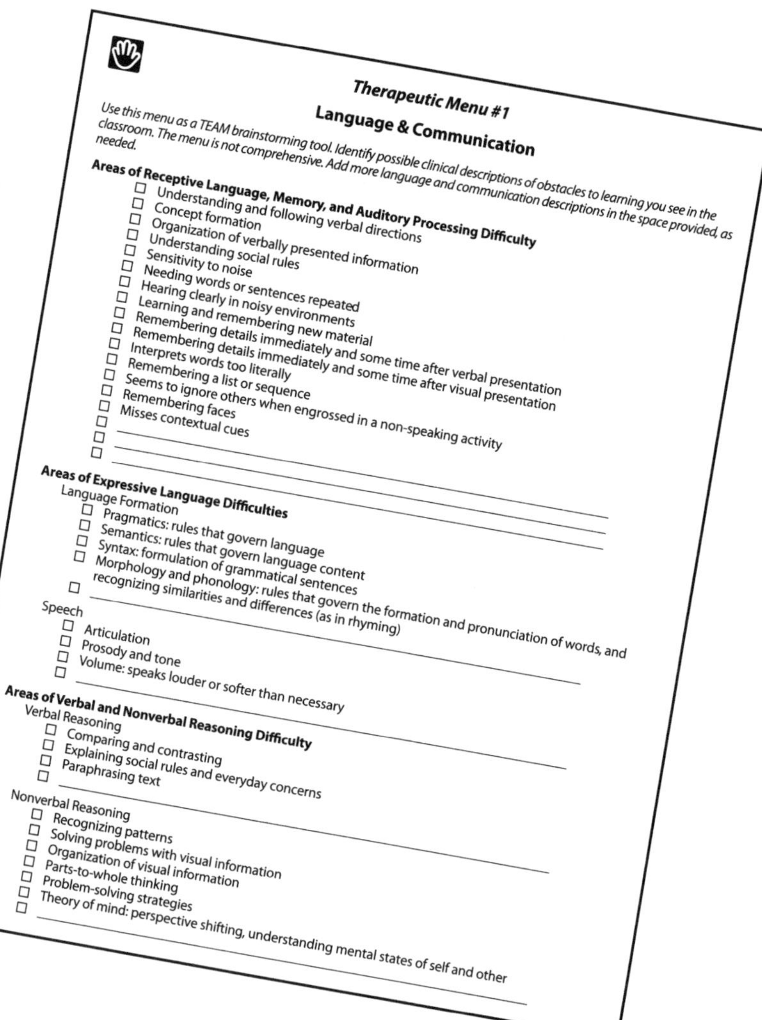

Therapeutic Menu #1

Language & Communication

Use this menu as a TEAM brainstorming tool. Identify possible clinical descriptions of obstacles to learning you see in the classroom. The menu is not comprehensive. Add more language and communication descriptions in the space provided, as needed.

Areas of Receptive Language, Memory, and Auditory Processing Difficulty

- ☐ Understanding and following verbal directions
- ☐ Concept formation
- ☐ Organization of verbally presented information
- ☐ Understanding social rules
- ☐ Sensitivity to noise
- ☐ Needing words or sentences repeated
- ☐ Hearing clearly in noisy environments
- ☐ Learning and remembering new material
- ☐ Remembering details immediately and some time after verbal presentation
- ☐ Remembering details immediately and some time after visual presentation
- ☐ Interprets words too literally
- ☐ Remembering a list or sequence
- ☐ Seems to ignore others when engrossed in a non-speaking activity
- ☐ Remembering faces
- ☐ Misses contextual cues
- ☐ ______
- ☐ ______

Areas of Expressive Language Difficulties

Language Formation

- ☐ Pragmatics: rules that govern language
- ☐ Semantics: rules that govern language content
- ☐ Syntax: formulation of grammatical sentences
- ☐ Morphology and phonology: rules that govern the formation and pronunciation of words, and recognizing similarities and differences (as in rhyming)
- ☐ ______

Speech

- ☐ Articulation
- ☐ Prosody and tone
- ☐ Volume: speaks louder or softer than necessary
- ☐ ______

Areas of Verbal and Nonverbal Reasoning Difficulty

Verbal Reasoning

- ☐ Comparing and contrasting
- ☐ Explaining social rules and everyday concerns
- ☐ Paraphrasing text
- ☐ ______

Nonverbal Reasoning

- ☐ Recognizing patterns
- ☐ Solving problems with visual information
- ☐ Organization of visual information
- ☐ Parts-to-whole thinking
- ☐ Problem-solving strategies
- ☐ Theory of mind: perspective shifting, understanding mental states of self and other
- ☐ ______

Exercise 1

Obstacles to Learning	***Possible Clinical Descriptions***
Constantly forgets instructions	______
Resists changing topics	______
Never asks for help	______

Perhaps, as you reviewed the menu for the obstacle "constantly forgets instructions," the clinical description "organization of verbally presented information" caught your eye. Of course, what you choose from the menu will depend upon the student or group of students you are considering. There might even be additional items on the menu that looked "appetizing" too, but sticking with the one that stands out most is a good beginning. It may turn out to be an important start in identifying an issue to target in your lesson plan.

(To see the full Language & Communication Menu, turn to page 65 of the Appendix or refer to the CD included with this book.)

Attention & Executive Function Menu

This menu could look like a job description for a bank manager. This is because many of the skills necessary to be an effective manager are contained in the functions we associate with this descriptive category, including

1. Planning
2. Organizational skills
3. Managing systems
4. Thinking across time

In fact, you might say that the *Lesson Plan a la Carte* system is itself an executive function aid designed to support many of the areas described in this category! These are key skills for success for any student and an area that many of our students have challenges in. See if you can choose some possible clinical descriptions for the obstacles to learning listed below by choosing items from this menu.

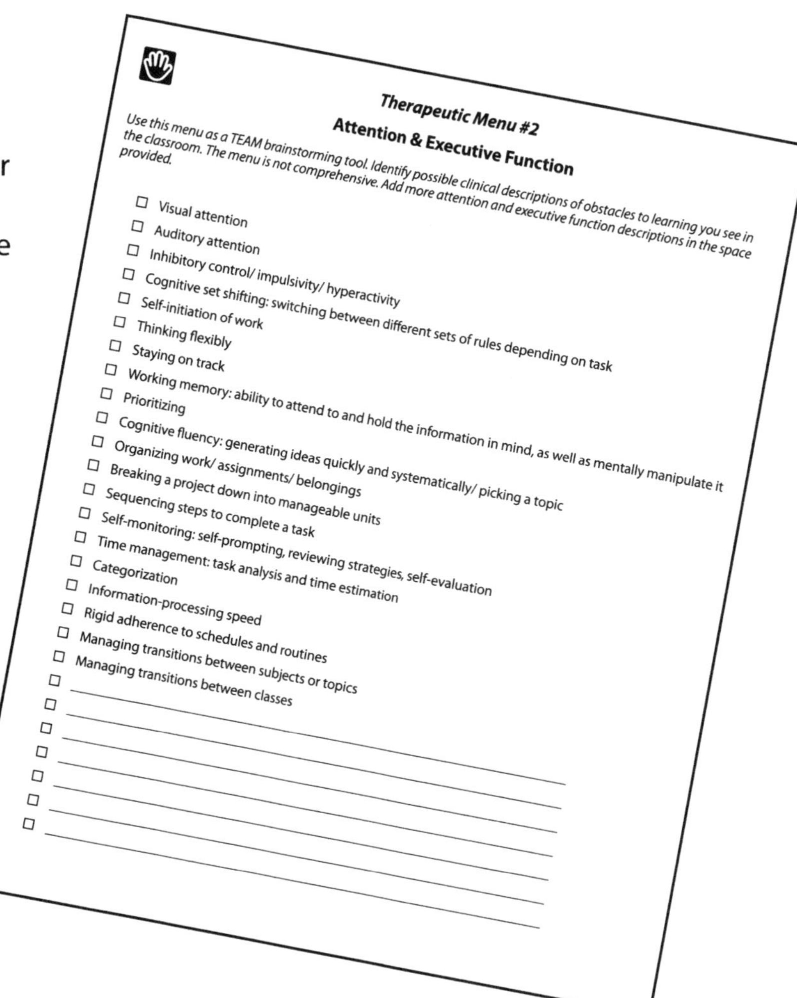

Therapeutic Menu #2

Attention & Executive Function

Use this menu as a TEAM brainstorming tool. Identify possible clinical descriptions of obstacles to learning you see in the classroom. The menu is not comprehensive. Add more attention and executive function descriptions in the space provided.

- ☐ Visual attention
- ☐ Auditory attention
- ☐ Inhibitory control/ impulsivity/ hyperactivity
- ☐ Cognitive set shifting: switching between different sets of rules depending on task
- ☐ Self-initiation of work
- ☐ Thinking flexibly
- ☐ Staying on track
- ☐ Working memory: ability to attend to and hold the information in mind, as well as mentally manipulate it
- ☐ Prioritizing
- ☐ Cognitive fluency: generating ideas quickly and systematically/ picking a topic
- ☐ Organizing work/ assignments/ belongings
- ☐ Breaking a project down into manageable units
- ☐ Sequencing steps to complete a task
- ☐ Self-monitoring: self-prompting, reviewing strategies, self-evaluation
- ☐ Time management: task analysis and time estimation
- ☐ Categorization
- ☐ Information-processing speed
- ☐ Rigid adherence to schedules and routines
- ☐ Managing transitions between subjects or topics
- ☐ Managing transitions between classes
- ☐ ________
- ☐ ________
- ☐ ________
- ☐ ________
- ☐ ________
- ☐ ________
- ☐ ________
- ☐ ________

Exercise 2

Obstacles to Learning	***Possible Clinical Descriptions***
Constantly losing school supplies & books	________
Always "zoning out"	________
Rarely or never turns in assignments	________

With time, you'll find that using the therapeutic menus becomes more than just an exercise. In fact, it is an important point in the planning process where clinical and educational perspectives are bridged and come to enrich each other. Once you have identified key clinical descriptions, both clinicians and teachers can focus on key issues (or therapeutic targets) as you write the lesson plan.

(To see the full Attention & Executive Function Menu, turn to page 66 of the Appendix or refer to the CD included with this book.)

Social & Emotional Menu

We've divided this menu into social difficulties and emotionally based difficulties.

Social difficulties are often particular to the specific context of the classroom, school, and/or community in which they occur. As you did before, try using the sample menu to the right to describe the following obstacles to learning.

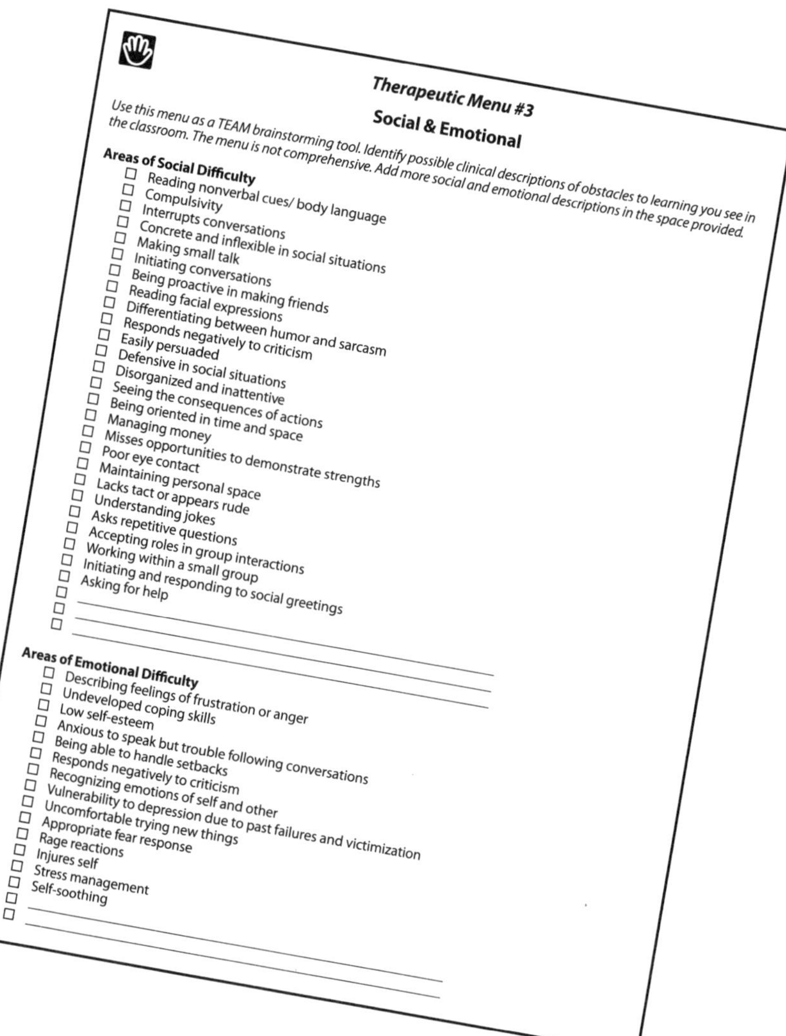

Therapeutic Menu #3

Social & Emotional

Use this menu as a TEAM brainstorming tool. Identify possible clinical descriptions of obstacles to learning you see in the classroom. The menu is not comprehensive. Add more social and emotional descriptions in the space provided.

Areas of Social Difficulty

- ☐ Reading nonverbal cues/ body language
- ☐ Compulsivity
- ☐ Interrupts conversations
- ☐ Concrete and inflexible in social situations
- ☐ Making small talk
- ☐ Initiating conversations
- ☐ Being proactive in making friends
- ☐ Reading facial expressions
- ☐ Differentiating between humor and sarcasm
- ☐ Responds negatively to criticism
- ☐ Easily persuaded
- ☐ Defensive in social situations
- ☐ Disorganized and inattentive
- ☐ Seeing the consequences of actions
- ☐ Being oriented in time and space
- ☐ Managing money
- ☐ Misses opportunities to demonstrate strengths
- ☐ Poor eye contact
- ☐ Maintaining personal space
- ☐ Lacks tact or appears rude
- ☐ Understanding jokes
- ☐ Asks repetitive questions
- ☐ Accepting roles in group interactions
- ☐ Working within a small group
- ☐ Initiating and responding to social greetings
- ☐ Asking for help
- ☐ ____________________
- ☐ ____________________
- ☐ ____________________

Areas of Emotional Difficulty

- ☐ Describing feelings of frustration or anger
- ☐ Undeveloped coping skills
- ☐ Low self-esteem
- ☐ Anxious to speak but trouble following conversations
- ☐ Being able to handle setbacks
- ☐ Responds negatively to criticism
- ☐ Recognizing emotions of self and other
- ☐ Vulnerability to depression due to past failures and victimization
- ☐ Uncomfortable trying new things
- ☐ Appropriate fear response
- ☐ Rage reactions
- ☐ Injures self
- ☐ Stress management
- ☐ Self-soothing
- ☐ ____________________
- ☐ ____________________
- ☐ ____________________

Exercise 3

Obstacles to Learning	***Possible Clinical Descriptions***
Students don't listen to each other	____________________
Always talks about special (deep) interests	____________________
Has meltdowns and can't work	____________________

(To see the full Social & Emotional Menu, turn to page 67 of the Appendix or refer to the CD included with this book.)

Sensory & Regulatory Menu

It has been estimated that up to two thirds of children and youth with ASD have emotional and social difficulties or problems related to their sensory processing.[11] For children with behavioral difficulties, significant sensory sensitivities are often found to be underlying their behavior problems. Many students with learning differences have clear strengths and weaknesses in one or more areas of sensory processing that, if identified and targeted, could vastly improve their access to learning. One example is difficulty in visual processing, which, because of its importance in classroom learning activities, we give its own subcategory.

Other areas in this menu focus on the ways in which motor coordination and sensory processing difficulties can affect a student's functioning. Now consider the following obstacles to learning as they relate to sensory and regulatory functions. Try to identify some possible underlying causes in the list of menu items that would clinically describe these obstacles.

Therapeutic Menu #4

Sensory & Regulatory

Use this menu as a TEAM brainstorming tool. Identify possible clinical descriptions of obstacles to learning you see in the classroom. The menu is not comprehensive. Add more sensory and regulatory descriptions as the team identifies them.

Areas of Visual Processing Difficulty

Spatial Relationships
- ☐ Ability to perceive words and numbers as separate units
- ☐ Directionality problems
- ☐ Confusion of similarly shaped letters, such as b/d or p/q
- ☐ ______

Visual Discrimination
- ☐ Ability to identify differences between objects
- ☐ Ability to recognize an object as distinct from its surrounding environment
- ☐ Ability to use visually presented material in a productive way
- ☐ ______

Visual Closure
- ☐ Ability to identify or recognize a symbol or object when the entire object is not visible
- ☐ ______

Whole/Part relationships
- ☐ Perceiving or integrating the relationship between an object (or symbol) in its entirety and the component parts that make it up
- ☐ ______

Areas of Motor Coordination

Gross Motor
- ☐ Bilateral integration: ability to use two sides of the body together
- ☐ Gravitational insecurity: an emotional or fear reaction that is out of proportion to the actual threat regarding position in space
- ☐ Balance
- ☐ Intolerance or aversive response to movement
- ☐ Motor planning: producing projected action sequences
- ☐ Strength and postural tone/stability issues
- ☐ Kinesthesia: awareness of body position in space
- ☐ ______

Fine Motor
- ☐ Grasp
- ☐ Manipulation: unilateral and/or bimanual
- ☐ Graphomotor
- ☐ Tactile discrimination
- ☐ ______

Other Areas of Sensory Processing

Sensory Over-Responsivity or Under-Responsivity
- ☐ Having a high or low threshold for touch, taste, smell, hearing, vision, body movement (proprioception), and/or head position and movement in space (vestibular)
- ☐ ______

Sensory Modulation
- ☐ Ability to down-regulate or up-regulate to maintain an optimal balance between attending to relevant stimuli and screening out unnecessary input
- ☐ May seek stimuli to point of distraction or self-injury
- ☐ May avoid stimuli to point of non-participation in activity
- ☐ ______

Exercise 4

Obstacles to Learning	***Possible Clinical Descriptions***
Refuses to fill out worksheets	______
Constantly shutting off lights	______
Constantly "zoning out"	______

(To see the full Sensory & Regulatory Menu, turn to page 68 of the Appendix or refer to the CD included with this book.)

11 Myles, B. S., Cook, K. T., Miller, N. E., Rinner, L., & Robbins, L. (2000). *Asperger Syndrome and Sensory Issues.* Shawnee Mission, KS: AAPC Publishing.

Using the Considerations for Planning Menus

While the four Therapeutic Menus are used to brainstorm and pinpoint possible clinical descriptions or underlying causes for obstacles to learning, and to enrich our understanding of the obstacles, another set of menus called Considerations for Planning assist us in the actual writing of the lesson plan. These menus are composed of lists of environmental, instructional, or other considerations you might wish to include when the lesson is implemented.

Considerations for Planning

Use the menus below as you write the DRAFT Integrated Lesson Plan in TEAM or SOLO planning. Identify relevant environmental, instructional, or additional considerations to keep in mind when the lesson plan is implemented. Some examples of strategies for implementation are offered below. The Considerations for Planning Menus and the strategy examples are not comprehensive; they are meant as a guide for developing strategies specific to your students and classroom as you write the DRAFT Integrated Lesson Plan. The team may add more considerations and strategies for implementation to the menus below where space is provided, creating a library of options that school personnel can tap into.

1. **Considerations for the Learning Environment**	1. **Implementation Strategies: Learning Environment**
• Eliminate distractions and consider where students' focus is drawn	• Close doors, remove distracting posters or images from classroom, avoid use of air fresheners or perfume, reduce or eliminate the use of fluorescent lighting
• Vary learning positions	• Offer seating and positioning alternatives (e.g., therapy ball, sitting on floor, lying down, sitting backwards on chair,

As you read through the Considerations for Planning Menus, picking and choosing *a la carte* which strategies and considerations should be included in your lesson plan, you will arrive at a total lesson plan that achieves the goal of this model: an integrated lesson that combines learning objectives with therapeutic supports and modifications directly in your classroom in the moment of instruction.

Let's look at a few samples from the Considerations for Planning Menus to acquaint you with their look and purpose. Remember, these menus are meant as a guide for developing strategies specific to your students and classroom as you draft your lesson plan. Here, for example, is a section from the menus devoted to Considerations for the Learning Environment:

1. **Considerations for the Learning Environment**	1. **Implementation Strategies: Learning Environment**
• Eliminate distractions and consider where students' focus is drawn	• Close doors, remove distracting posters or images from classroom, avoid use of air fresheners or perfume, reduce or eliminate the use of fluorescent lighting
• Vary learning positions	• Offer seating and positioning alternatives (e.g., therapy ball, sitting on floor, lying down, sitting backwards on chair, standing)
• Create space to regulate arousal (up-regulate* or down-regulate*)	• Offer short breaks in a calm, quiet environment, a quiet room, or the hallway; alternatively a place to up-regulate or get re-energized, like a place to take a walk or jump on a trampoline)
• Reduce overstimulation but maximize social integration	• Arrange student seating
• Facilitate greater autonomy	• Ensure that learning spaces are organized and visually labeled

In the left-hand column, you'll find a menu of suggestions, such as "eliminate distractions and consider where students' focus is drawn." Beside each consideration, in the right-hand column, are suggested implementation strategies. In this instance, one suggested strategy is "close doors, remove distracting posters or images from classroom, avoid use of air fresheners or perfume, reduce or eliminate the use of fluorescent lighting."

Here is another example from the Considerations for Planning Menu focusing on social and emotional considerations:

5. **Considerations for Further Social & Emotional Enhancements**	5. **Implementation Strategies: Social & Emotional**
• Facilitate peer relationships that provide opportunities for mentorship and modeling	• Establish a "partner classroom" with a general ed classroom
• Provide supports for team or group work	• Use scripting, delineating, and modeling of roles
• Vary group size according to need	• Use larger group games for teambuilding fun, paired work for collaboration (limit academic work done in groups of 3 or 4)
• Generalize modifications and teaching strategies for the entire class	• Remember that most strategies are beneficial to the entire class

In the left-hand column, one consideration for planning listed is "develop a set of discreet cues for teacher-student communication" with a possible implementation strategy being "use cards or hand signals" or "for emergency movement breaks* or redirection, send student on an errand." One thing is clear, as educators we cannot possibly keep the rich array of planning options in our heads as we go through our daily lesson planning processes. The Considerations for Planning Menus help us quickly move through a broad set of options, so that we can pick and choose what serves us best in a particular lesson or teaching moment, thereby enriching the design of the lesson.

(Complete versions of the Considerations for Planning Menus are located on page 69 of the Appendix, or refer to the CD included with this book.)

If the strategies listed aren't the precise solution for your particular student(s), use them as a guide to assist you in discovering your own solutions and strategies. In this way, the Considerations for Planning Menu is not meant to be comprehensive. In fact, there is space provided in the menus to add more considerations and strategies that you or your team discover and develop along the way.

CHAPTER 3

GETTING TO KNOW THE TEMPLATES

Two Planning Methods for Flexible Options: TEAM and SOLO

The templates carry you through the key stages of brainstorming, drafting, and finalizing your lesson plan, whether you work in a solo or team fashion. Guided instructions are printed right on the template forms. Each time you or your team want to write a new lesson plan, you'll work your way through a fresh series of these templates, clearly identified as SOLO or TEAM, depending upon your work process. (See pages 83-91 for complete sets of template systems or refer to the CD included with this book.)

Walkthrough: *Lesson Plan a la Carte* TEAM

The TEAM planning templates guide your team by structuring a group planning process through brainstorming, drafting, and finalizing the integrated lesson plan. You will make use of both the Therapeutic Menus and the Considerations for Planning Menus as you construct a lesson. The TEAM planning method can be used at all levels of team intervention, whether to modify existing curriculum, develop new curriculum, or address the needs of a specific student or group of students. (For complete sets of planning templates for TEAM, see the Appendix on pages 84-88 or the CD included with this book.)

STEP 1: TEAM Brainstorming

1. Learning Objective

Name: ________________
Date: ________________
Class/Teacher: ________________
Unit: ________________

Lesson Plan a la Carte
TEAM Planning Step 1

TEAM Brainstorming

1 Introduce Learning Objective

The initiating teacher or therapist briefly presents the learning objective(s).

Introduction to the concept of reducing as it relates to students' personal responsibility to the environments around them.

1. Name or Description of Lesson
Enter the name or a brief description of the lesson here. This description will likely change once you have moved through more of the steps of planning. Don't worry about making it perfect now. You can do that in the final lesson-planning template of this series.

Tip: This might be a lesson you are teaching for the first time, or one you have taught several times. Alternatively, your team might be working together to develop a specialized curriculum. This template set serves all of these purposes.

2. Identify Obstacles to Learning and Possible Clinical Descriptions

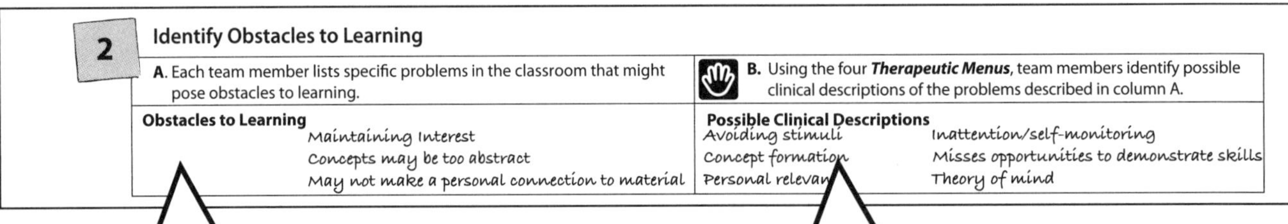

2 Identify Obstacles to Learning

A. Each team member lists specific problems in the classroom that might pose obstacles to learning.	**B.** Using the four ***Therapeutic Menus***, team members identify possible clinical descriptions of the problems described in column A.	
Obstacles to Learning	**Possible Clinical Descriptions**	
Maintaining interest	Avoiding stimuli	Inattention/self-monitoring
Concepts may be too abstract	Concept formation	Misses opportunities to demonstrate skills
May not make a personal connection to material	Personal relevan[ce]	Theory of mind

2A. Obstacles to Learning
Include specific obstacles to learning here. These can be drawn from a student's BIP or other target behaviors, or they can be included here out of sheer necessity because they are challenges that you and the student(s) are currently facing.

2B. Possible Clinical Descriptions
Having narrowed your list down to two or three obstacles to learning, you're now ready to utilize the Therapeutic Menus (pp. 64-68). Consider your obstacles to learning, review each of the four Therapeutic Menus, and list possible clinical descriptions of those obstacles.

Tip: You can structure team meetings using the planning templates. For example, once you have completed parts A and B shown above, team members can take turns to share their results from using the menus. You don't have to be a clinician to use the menus. The menus act as a bridge between the teaching and clinical experience, providing built-in staff development as you work together.

Tip: It's good to choose someone on the team to run the meeting, guiding everyone through each of the planning steps outlined on the templates. That way, you all stay on the same page.

Tip: Consider having one team member take notes, or to keep a master copy of the planning templates, so that you have both working and final versions you can turn to again.

3. Identify Therapeutic Target Areas & Brainstorm Integrated Lesson Ideas

3 Identify Therapeutic Target Areas & Brainstorm Integrated Lesson Ideas

A. Team members briefly present their answers from columns A and B above. Using this information, the team identifies the most relevant areas of difficulty to target with therapeutic intervention(s).	**B.** Next, the team brainstorms lesson ideas that integrate therapeutic interventions with learning objectives.
Areas to Target With Therapeutic Intervention(s)	**Integrated Lesson Ideas**
Concept formation Personal relevance Inattention/self-monitoring	Introduce concept of reduce using group activities and games that involve reducing numbers of people or objects such that you end up with only what is necessary. Go to supermarket or other community establishment to see what can be reduced. Create and teach use of home material that includes a "tip of the day" and/or a chart to monitor energy use.

3A. Areas to Target With Therapeutic Interventions
From the list of clinical descriptions, choose two or three to focus on and list them here.

3B. Integrated Lesson Ideas
Here each team member has an opportunity to reflect on the initial learning objective(s) and the therapeutic targets. The goal is to jot down ideas for addressing both in an integrated lesson plan.

Tip: Don't get caught up in writing the entire lesson plan itself at this point. One or two ideas from here may ultimately be used by your team, or a sketch of a lesson might emerge. Simply jot down notes for a proposed integrated lesson here.

4. Name the Lesson, Choose Author(s)

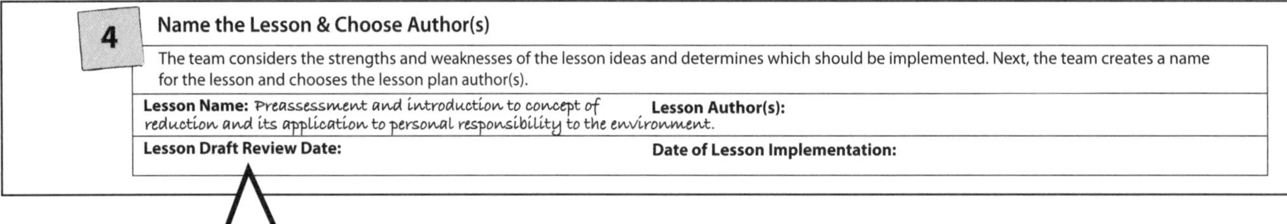

4

Name the Lesson & Choose Author(s)

The team considers the strengths and weaknesses of the lesson ideas and determines which should be implemented. Next, the team creates a name for the lesson and chooses the lesson plan author(s).

Lesson Name: Preassessment and introduction to concept of reduction and its application to personal responsibility to the environment.	**Lesson Author(s):**
Lesson Draft Review Date:	**Date of Lesson Implementation:**

4. Name the Lesson, Choose Author(s)
Write down a revised lesson name or brief description of the lesson that takes into account the integrated focus. Decide who is going to draft the lesson, when the lesson draft will be available to be reviewed by the team, and when the lesson will be taught.

Tip: Remember to have a records keeper on the team who ensures that plans are completed on time and filed in one place for all to refer to.

STEP 2: TEAM Draft

1. Name and Brief Description of Lesson

Name: ____________________
Date: ____________________
Class/Teacher: ____________________
Unit: ____________________

Lesson Plan a la Carte
TEAM Planning Step 2

TEAM Draft Lesson Plan

Lesson Author(s):	**Date of Lesson Implementation:**

1. Name & Brief Description of the Lesson:

Preassessment and introduction to the concept of reducing as it relates to students' personal responsibility to the environments around them.

1. Name and Brief Description of Lesson
Restate the lesson name or description and add any detail necessary to clarify the terms and intent.

2. Learning Objectives, Essential Questions & Skills

2. Learning Objective(s):

Define reduction
Demonstrate understanding of reduction
Assess current understanding of the concept of reduction both outside and within the context of environmental awareness

2. Learning Objectives
Here you can restate, and if useful, elaborate on the important elements of the original learning objective(s).

3. Therapeutic Target Areas

3. Therapeutic Target Areas:
Restate the therapeutic target areas your team chose here.

3. Therapeutic Target Areas:

Concept formation
Personal relevance
Inattention/self-monitoring

4. Considerations for Planning

4. Considerations for Planning: Turn to the Menu of Considerations for Planning and list any relevant items the team should do or keep in mind during implementation.

Preassessment

Break task instructions down

Assign roles to students during small-group activities

Give guidelines for sharing during initial brainstorming

Show people doing positive things

4. Considerations for Planning
Referring to the items listed in the left-hand column of Considerations for Planning Menus (pp. 69-78), determine how you will implement the lesson. In other words, use this list as a guide for identifying the things you will need to consider in order to address your students' social-emotional, language-communication, sensory-regulatory, or organizational needs.

Tip: It's a good idea to limit yourself to no more than three items from the Considerations for Planning Menus. That way, when you implement the lesson plan, you will be able provide focus to your teaching and work more effectively in integrating supports and accommodations. Choosing too many items from the menu is a lot like ordering too much in a restaurant. The result: Neither you nor your student(s) will be able to digest it all in one sitting.

5. Implementation Strategies

5. Implementation Strategies
In this section, your selected Considerations for Planning become transformed into actual activities or methods you'll implement in the classroom. At this point, you are not writing up all the steps of implementation, but are beginning to assemble the pieces for it. For suggestions on implementation strategies, look at the right-hand column of the Considerations for Planning Menus that corresponds with each item you listed in box 4. Keep in mind, these items are only suggestions and are in no way comprehensive. You might end up creating your own strategies to insert in this section of the plan, and there is space provided in the Considerations for Planning Menus to add new strategies.

5. Implementation Strategies: For each item you listed as a Consideration for Planning, provide details on how you will integrate these considerations into the lesson plan.

Use a graphic organizer* or computer program to structure and document preassessment

Provide specific instructions prior to tasks

Provide specific questions for students to focus on when considering the concept of reducing

6. Supporting Materials

6. Supporting Materials: If implementation of the lesson will require supporting materials, list them here. Supporting materials might include emotion charts, graphic organizers*, fidgets, Power Cards*, etc.)

Gum, fidgets, putty, adapted pencils, "Handwriting Without Tears" paper for some students, picture prompts, rules written down, projector, laptop

6. Supporting Materials
These are all the materials you will need to gather or prepare in advance, in order to implement the lesson.

7. Implementation

Name:________________
Date:________________
Class/Teacher:________________
Unit:________________

Lesson Plan a la Carte
TEAM Planning Step 2

TEAM Draft Lesson Plan Cont.

7. Implementation: Divide the lesson into discrete activities, describing each step deliberately. Next to the activity description, list the specific implementation strategies and supporting materials the team will use, and clearly indicate who will take the lead in each step. Be certain that each staff member in the classroom has a defined role, including teachers, therapists, paraprofessionals, and assistants. Students need this clarity in order to be successful.

Activity	Strategies for Implementation	Supporting Materials	Lead & Team Supports
1. Preassessment activity	Preassessment graphic organizer* Establish clear rules	Gum, fidgets, putty, adapted pencils, "Handwriting Without Tears" paper for some students, picture prompts, rules written	Teacher leads Teacher assistant and paraeducator assist in scribing/writing for some

7. Implementation
In this section of the template, sketch out all the steps of implementing the lesson, filling in each column as it applies. Once completed, you can review the draft with the team and add any final revisions. If more than one educator is in the room, be sure to point out who will be doing what during each segment of lesson implementation.

8. Review Notes and Suggestions

8. Review Notes & Suggestions: As the team reviews the draft lesson plan, note additional suggestions or improvements for the final draft.
Utilize a self-regulation scale to help students self-monitor and remain engaged.
Form groups with one student in each group capable of facilitating the brainstorming process.
Utilize an "island hopping" format. Each staff member runs a group and the students move from group to group.

8. Review Notes & Suggestions
This section is a prompt to remember to take notes as team members review and provide feedback on the draft plan. Highlight important updates here.

9. School Documentation and Protocols

9. School Documentation & Protocols: The team notes any mandated or IEP-driven goals and related services that might be addressed or satisfied by the lesson plan.
Send copy of final lesson plan to IEP lead/homeroom teacher. Provide copy of lesson plan to a family as basis of meeting during parent-teacher conference.

9. School Documentation and Protocols
This section of the lesson plan is meant to support you and your program or school in providing documentation for any aspect of your responsibilities in reporting that you, your team, or your supervisors devise.

STEP 3: TEAM Lesson Plan

1. **Name and Brief Description of the Lesson**
2. **Learning Objectives**
3. **Therapeutic Targets**

Name:
Date:
Class/Teacher:
Unit:

Lesson Plan a la Carte
TEAM Planning Step 3

TEAM Lesson Plan

Each person in the classroom receives a double-sided copy of this plan.

INTEGRATED LESSON PLAN | **Date of Implementation:**

1. Name & Brief Description of the Lesson:
Preassessment and ntroduction to the concept of reducing as it relates to students' personal responsibility to the environments around them.

2. Learning Objective(s):	3. Therapeutic Target Areas:
Define reduction	Concept formation
Demonstrate understanding of reduction	Personal relevance
Assess students' current understanding of the concept of reduction both outside and within the context of environ-	Inattention/self-monitoring

6. ASSESSMENT **Date:**

Rate the Lesson
On a scale of 1 to 5, rate how you feel the lesson generally went.
1 2 3 4 (5)
poorly okay very well
Notes:
The students were far more engaged in this lesson than they typically are.

Learning Objectives & Therapeutic Targets
Were the Learning Objectives

Tip: Transferring this information into the final lesson plan allows everyone who reads the plan to implement the plan consistently.

1-3. Restate the Basic Information
On the TEAM Lesson Plan template, restate the lesson name, learning objectives and therapeutic targets, and add any necessary detail to clarify the terms and intent.

4. Implementation

4. Implementation

Activity	Strategies for Implementation	Supporting Materials	Lead & Team Supports
1. Quick gauge of everyone's regulatory level followed by preassessment activity	Preassessment graphic organizer* Establish clear rules	Gum, fidgets, putty, adapted pencils, "Handwriting Without Tears" paper for some students,	Teacher leads Teacher assistant and paraeducator assist in scribing/writing for some students

Were the Therapeutic Target Areas addressed?
☐ no ☐ partially ☑ yes
Notes:
As the teacher, I feel that my learning objectives were met.

Considerations for Planning

4. Implementation
In this section of the template, sketch out all the steps of implementing the lesson, filling in each column as it applies. Once completed, you can hand out the final lesson plan to anyone working with you in the classroom (such as a paraprofessional or a student teacher). This keeps everyone on the same page during the various steps of the lesson, and provides students with an organized presentation. If more than one educator is in the room, be sure to point out who is doing what during each segment of lesson implementation.

5. School Documentation and Protocols

5. School Documentation & Protocols

Send copy of final lesson plan to IEP lead/homeroom teacher. Provide copy of lesson plan to family as basis of meeting during parent/teacher conference.

Sent copy of lesson plan, along with assessment results, to main office to be filed with other integrated lessons for future review and use.

5. School Documentation and Protocols
This section of the lesson plan is meant to support you and your program or school in providing documentation for any aspect of your responsibilities in reporting that you, your team, or your supervisors devise.

Tip: You might also wish to use this lesson plan as documentation for any of the following:

- Substantiating IEP goal progress
- Demonstrating how SDIs are implemented
- Tracking RTI for 1st, 2nd, or 3rd tier intervention
- Substantiating DDD
- Providing to your supervisors, as part of an observation/evaluation of your teaching
- Presenting to your school board or board of directors
- Sharing with parents/families

6. Assessment

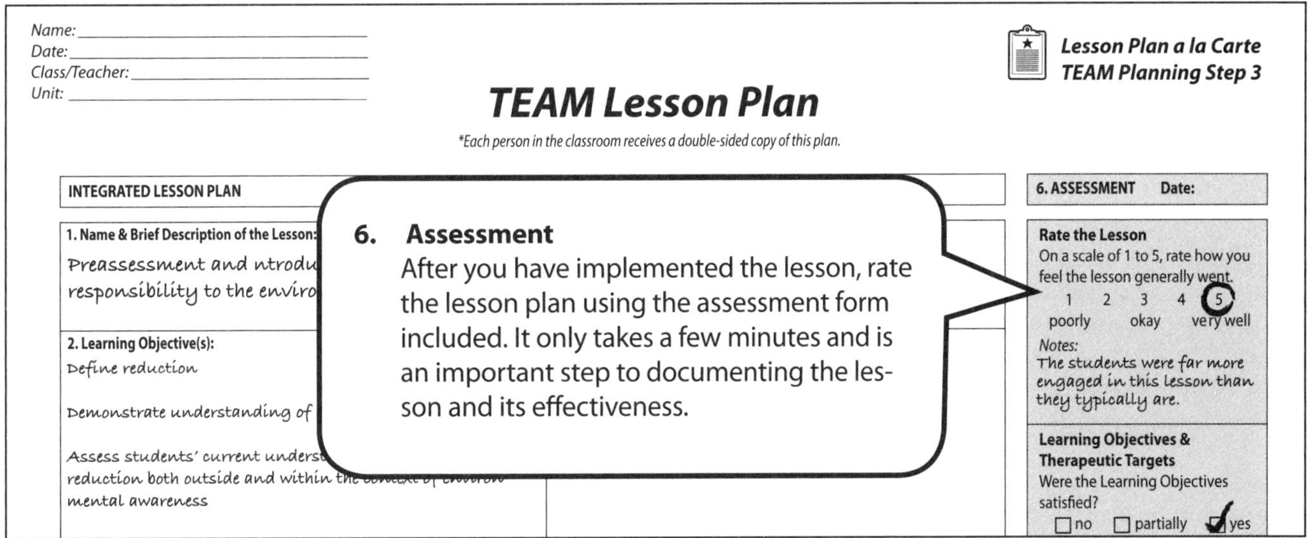

Tip: Have each educator in the classroom complete his or her own assessment on his or her copy of the lesson plan and save everyone's copies for documentation and future reference.

Walkthrough: *Lesson Plan a la Carte* SOLO

The SOLO planning method is designed specifically for teachers who are writing lesson plans on their own, with little or no collaborative support from other teachers or therapists. The SOLO method can be very useful, for example, if you're a teacher in a general education setting who is integrating one or more students with IEPs or 504 plans, or if you are co-teaching with a special educator but have little time for shared planning.

You likely have lesson plans for the class already, or at least a curriculum map or textbooks that dictate what you must teach. The SOLO planning system guides you through a process of modifying a lesson so as to integrate students with sensory, environmental, and communication needs more seamlessly into your instruction. In essence, you are documenting HOW you're doing just that in your lesson plans. (For complete sets of planning templates for SOLO, see the Appendix on pages 89-91 or the CD included with this book).

STEP 1: SOLO Draft

1. Name and Brief Description of the Lesson

Name:
Date:
Class/Teacher:
Unit:

Lesson Plan a la Carte
SOLO Planning Step 1

SOLO Draft Lesson Plan

Lesson Author:	Date of Lesson Implementation:

1. Name & Brief Description of the Lesson:
7th-grade science lab: the germination of seeds; experiment setup

2. Learning Objective(s): Students will lear[n] to follow lab directions for setting up germination experiment. [Stu]dents will draft designs for data tables to demonstrate d[...]tion over time (3-week period), with at least 2 quantitative [...] be documented in the data tables. Students	**3. Obstacles to Learning:** List specific problems in the classroom that might pose obstacles to learning. Even though her individual class work is good, Mary does poorly in labs when she has to collaborate with fellow students.

1. Name the Lesson
Enter the name or a brief description of the lesson here. This description will likely change once you have moved through more of the steps of planning. Don't worry about making it perfect now. You can do that in the final lesson-planning template of this series.

2. Learning Objective(s)

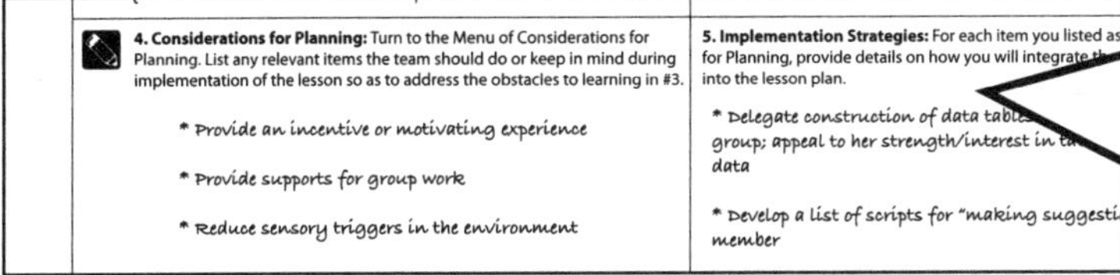

4. Considerations for Planning: Turn to the Menu of Considerations for Planning. List any relevant items the team should do or keep in mind during implementation of the lesson so as to address the obstacles to learning in #3.	**5. Implementation Strategies:** For each item you listed as [...] for Planning, provide details on how you will integrate [...] into the lesson plan.
* Provide an incentive or motivating experience * Provide supports for group work * Reduce sensory triggers in the environment	* Delegate construction of data tabl[...] group; appeal to her strength/interest in [...] data * Develop a list of scripts for "making suggesti[...] member

2. Learning Objective(s)
Enter the learning objectives you will teach to, or have taught to in the past, when implementing this lesson. This section will probably change once you have moved through the steps of integrated planning in this draft. Don't worry about making it perfect now! You can do that in the final lesson planning template.

> **Tip:** If you are a general education teacher, this might be a lesson you have taught several times. The point here is to write down as objectives what you would normally teach to. When you reach your final lesson plan objectives, you will likely find what you have written here more enhanced, in order to support one or more students with special needs in your classroom.

3. Obstacles to Learning

3. Obstacles to Learning
Include specific obstacles to learning here. These can be drawn from a student's BIP or other target behaviors, or they can be included here out of sheer necessity because they are challenges that you and the student(s) are currently facing.

3. Obstacles to Learning: List specific problems in the classroom that might pose obstacles to learning.

Even though her individual class work is good, Mary does poorly in labs when she has to collaborate with fellow students. She blurts out inappropriate remarks, interrupting class and other students.

Tip: In SOLO planning, the focus might be on one or a small group of IEP or 504 plan students. It's important not to attempt to address too many obstacles in one lesson plan. Prioritize which obstacle you wish to address first. Keep it simple. Allow yourself to focus. It makes life in the classroom easier and more productive for you and for your students.

4. Considerations for Planning

4. Considerations for Planning: Turn to the Menu of Considerations for Planning. List any relevant items the team should do or keep in mind during implementation of the lesson so as to address the obstacles to learning in #3.

* *Provide an incentive or motivating experience*
* *Provide supports for group work*
* *Reduce sensory triggers in the environment*

4. Considerations for Planning
Referring to the items listed in the left-hand column of Considerations for Planning Menus (pp. 69-78), determine how you will implement the lesson. In other words, use this list as a guide for identifying the things you will need to consider in order to address your students' social-emotional, language-communication, sensory-regulatory, or organizational needs.

Tip: It's a good idea to limit yourself to no more than three items from the Considerations for Planning Menus, that way, when you implement the lesson plan, you will be able provide focus to your teaching and work more effectively in integrating supports and accommodations. Choosing too many items from the menu is a lot like ordering too much in a restaurant. The result: Neither you nor your student(s) will be able to digest it all in one sitting.

5. Implementation Strategies

5. Implementation Strategies
In this section, your selected Considerations for Planning become transformed into actual activities or methods you'll implement in the classroom. At this point, you are not writing up all the steps of implementation but are beginning to assemble the pieces for it. For suggestions on implementation strategies, look at the right-hand column of the Considerations for Planning Menus that corresponds with each item you listed in box 4. Keep in mind, these items are only suggestions and are in no way comprehensive. You might end up creating your own strategies to insert in this section of the plan. There is space provided in the Considerations for Planning Menus to add new strategies.

5. Implementation Strategies: For each item you listed as a Consideration for Planning, provide details on how you will integrate these considerations into the lesson plan.

* Delegate construction of data tables to Mary as a task in her group; appeal to her strength/interest in tabulation, lists, and data

* Develop a list of scripts for "making suggestions" to a team member

* Assign Mary a screening role for lab materials. Ask her to collect data on dangers, sensory qualities, etc. Then present a

6. Supporting Materials

6. Supporting Materials: If implementation of the lesson will require supporting materials, list them here. Supporting materials might include emotion charts, graphic organizers, fidgets, Power Cards, etc.

Seed germination kits (seeds, paper towel, jars, plastic baggies, soil, paper cups, colored light bulbs); scripts for "making suggestions" to a team member; descriptions of lab roles and responsibilities

6. Supporting Materials
These are all the materials you will need to gather or prepare in advance in order to implement the lesson.

SOLO Lesson Plan

1. Name and Brief Description of the Lesson

Name: ______________________
Date: ______________________
Class/Teacher: ______________________
Unit: ______________________

Lesson Plan a la Carte
SOLO Planning Step 2

SOLO Lesson Plan

**Each staff in the classroom receives a double-sided copy of this plan.*

INTEGRATED LESSON PLAN	**Date of Implementation:**

1. Name & Brief Description of the Lesson:
Setting up a seed germination lab for observation and data collection. Students will work in groups of 2, taking on specific lab roles: (1) data collection design and (2) lab setup, with sensory accommodations and supports for successful group work.

5. ASSESSMENT **Date:**

Rate the Lesson
On a scale of 1 to 5, rate how you feel the lesson generally went
1 2 3 4 (5)

> **1. Name and Description of Lesson**
> Copy the name and description from your draft plan with any revisions if necessary.

2. Learning Objective(s)

2. Learning Objective(s):
Students will learn to follow lab directions for setting up germination and observation experiments. Students will learn how to cooperate and make suggestions to one another in a lab setting. Students will draft designs for data tables that show data collection over 3-week period, with at least 3 variables (temperature, light, soil, location, etc.). Students will learn the characteristics of qualitative and quantitative data and show examples in their data tables. Students will work within the lab roles they have been assigned.

Notes:
Mary responded very well to knowing her assigned role in the lab team. Written instructions helped her know her responsibilities and seemed to reduce stress. Also, the entire class benefited from this structure.

Learning Objectives

> **2. Learning Objective(s)**
> As in the draft lesson plan, write the learning objectives for the lesson here. Often, you will find that your learning objectives have evolved from the form they took in the draft template. This is because you have likely added new objectives in the process of making the plan more integrated.

> **Tip:** As a test, compare your learning objectives shown here with those delineated in the draft lesson plan above. Have they changed? If so, how?

3. Implementation

3. Implementation

Activity	Strategies for Implementation	Supporting Materials	Lead
Ask Mary to review lab materials during opening minutes of class	Provide supports for group work; provide an incentive or motivating experience; reduce sensory triggers in the environment	Kits include lab materials, plus descriptions of lab roles and responsibilities and scripts for	Teacher Teacher aide (while teacher is working with Mary)

Were the Learning Objectives satisfied?
☐ no ☐ partially ☑ yes

Notes:
All learning objectives were met for Mary and for the class in general. Each team completed lab setup and designed data tables, working well within their assigned lab roles. Many teams made use of the scripts for

> **3. Implementation**
> In this section of the template, sketch out all the steps of implementing the lesson, filling in each column as it applies. Once completed, you can hand out the final lesson plan to anyone working with you in the classroom (such as a paraprofessional or a student teacher). This keeps everyone on the same page during the various steps of the lesson and provides students with an organized presentation. If more than one educator is in the room, be sure to point out who is doing what during each segment of lesson implementation.

4. School Documentation and Protocols

4. School Documentation & Protocols

Send copy of final lesson plan with completed assessment to Mary's IEP lead/homeroom teacher. Provide copy of lesson plan to family as basis of meeting during parent-teacher conference.

Notes: no yes
Sent copy of lesson plan, along with assessment results, to Mary's homeroom/IEP teacher. Parent-teacher conference scheduled for 11/17/2010.

4. School Documentation and Protocols
This section of the lesson plan is meant to support you and your program or school in providing documentation for any aspect of your responsibilities in reporting that you, your team, or your supervisors devise.

Tip: You might also wish to use this lesson plan as documentation for any of the following:

- Substantiating IEP goal progress
- Demonstrating how SDIs are implemented
- Tracking RTI for 1st, 2nd or 3rd tier intervention
- Substantiating DDD
- Providing to your supervisors, as part of an observation/evaluation of your teaching
- Presenting to your school board or board of directors
- Sharing with parents/families

5. Assessment

5. ASSESSMENT Date:

Rate the Lesson
On a scale of 1 to 5, rate how you feel the lesson generally went.
1 2 3 4 5 (circled)
poorly okay very well
Notes:
Mary responded very well to knowing her assigned role in the lab team. Written instructions helped her know her responsibilities and seemed to reduce stress. Also, the entire class benefited from this structure.

Learning Objectives
Were the Learning Objectives satisfied?
☐ no ☐ partially ☑ yes
Notes:
All learning objectives were met for Mary and for the class in general. Each team completed lab setup and designed data tables, working well within their assigned lab roles. Many teams made use of the scripts for "making suggestions." Mary used the scripts several times throughout the lesson.

Considerations for Planning
Were the Considerations for Planning successfully considered or implemented?
☐ no ☐ partially ☑ yes
Notes:
In the future, it would be a good idea to take more time with Mary on preteaching in order to make her feel more comfortable and able to process the material to be covered.

ASSESSMENT Cont.

Staff Roles
Were staff roles during implementation clear & successfully executed?
☐ no ☐ partially ☑ yes
Notes:
The teacher assistant was more involved with students than in the past. She stepped in as planned, and I was able to delegate responsibility, particularly so that I could offer Mary 1:1 support in the opening minutes of the period.

Obstacles to Learning
Revisit the obstacles to learning that you identified your draft. Were the obstacles addressed by the lesson plan?
☐ no ☐ partially ☑ yes
Notes:
I have never seen Mary this integrated into class. She worked well with her partner and made no inappropriate remarks or comments that interrupted class. The overall plan helped the entire class to be more organized and work well in pairs.

Documentation
Will you use this lesson plan as evidence for documenting IEP fidelity, IEP goals, SDI, RTI or other mandates/protocols? ☐ ☑
Notes: no yes
Sent copy of lesson plan, along with assessment results, to Mary's homeroom/IEP teacher. Parent-teacher conference scheduled for 11/17/2010.

5. Assessment
After you have implemented the lesson, rate the lesson plan using the assessment form included.

TEAM Lesson Plan Examples

Name: ____________________
Date: ____________________
Class/Teacher: ____________________
Unit: ____________________

Lesson Plan a la Carte
TEAM Planning Step 1

TEAM Brainstorming

1 Introduce Learning Objective

The initiating teacher or therapist briefly presents the learning objective(s).
Introduction to the concept of reducing as it relates to students' personal responsibility to the environments around them.

2 Identify Obstacles to Learning

A. Each team member lists specific problems in the classroom that might pose obstacles to learning.	**B.** Using the four ***Therapeutic Menus***, team members identify possible clinical descriptions of the problems described in column A.
Obstacles to Learning *Maintaining interest* *Concepts may be too abstract* *May not make a personal connection to material*	**Possible Clinical Descriptions** *Avoiding stimuli* *Concept formation* *Personal relevance* *Inattention/self-monitoring* *Misses opportunities to demonstrate skills* *Theory of mind*

3 Identify Therapeutic Target Areas & Brainstorm Integrated Lesson Ideas

A. Team members briefly present their answers from columns A and B above. Using this information, the team identifies the most relevant areas of difficulty to target with therapeutic intervention(s).	**B.** Next, the team brainstorms lesson ideas that integrate therapeutic interventions with learning objectives.
Areas to Target With Therapeutic Intervention(s) *Concept formation* *Personal relevance* *Inattention/self-monitoring*	**Integrated Lesson Ideas** *Introduce concept of reduce using group activities and games that involve reducing numbers of people or objects such that you end up with only what is necessary.* *Go to supermarket or other community establishment to see what can be reduced.* *Create and teach use of home material that includes a "tip of the day" and/or a chart to monitor energy use.*

4 Name the Lesson & Choose Author(s)

The team considers the strengths and weaknesses of the lesson ideas and determines which should be implemented. Next, the team creates a name for the lesson and chooses the lesson plan author(s).

Lesson Name: *Preassessment and introduction to concept of reduction and its application to personal responsibility to the environment.* **Lesson Author(s):**

Lesson Draft Review Date: **Date of Lesson Implementation:**

Name: ____________________
Date: ____________________
Class/Teacher: ____________________
Unit: ____________________

Lesson Plan a la Carte
TEAM Planning Step 2

TEAM Draft Lesson Plan

Lesson Author(s): **Date of Lesson Implementation:**

1. Name & Brief Description of the Lesson:

Preassessment and introduction to the concept of reducing as it relates to students' personal responsibility to the environments around them.

2. Learning Objective(s):	**3. Therapeutic Target Areas:**
Define reduction Demonstrate understanding of reduction Assess current understanding of the concept of reduction both outside and within the context of environmental awareness	Concept formation Personal relevance Inattention/self-monitoring
4. Considerations for Planning: Turn to the Menu of Considerations for Planning and list any relevant items the team should do or keep in mind during implementation. Preassessment Break task instructions down Assign roles to students during small-group activities Give guidelines for sharing during initial brainstorming Show people doing positive things	**5. Implementation Strategies:** For each item you listed as a Consideration for Planning, provide details on how you will integrate these considerations into the lesson plan. Use a graphic organizer* or computer program to structure and document preassessment Provide specific instructions prior to tasks Provide specific questions for students to focus on when considering the concept of reducing

6. Supporting Materials: If implementation of the lesson will require supporting materials, list them here. Supporting materials might include emotion charts, graphic organizers*, fidgets, Power Cards*, etc.)

Gum, fidgets, putty, adapted pencils, "Handwriting Without Tears" paper for some students, picture prompts, rules written down, projector, laptop

Name: ____________
Date: ____________
Class/Teacher: ____________
Unit: ____________

Lesson Plan a la Carte
TEAM Planning Step 2

TEAM Draft Lesson Plan Cont.

7. Implementation: Divide the lesson into discrete activities, describing each step deliberately. Next to the activity description, list the specific implementation strategies and supporting materials the team will use, and clearly indicate who will take the lead in each step. Be certain that each staff member in the classroom has a defined role, including teachers, therapists, paraprofessionals, and assistants. Students need this clarity in order to be successful.

Activity	Strategies for Implementation	Supporting Materials	Lead & Team Supports
1. Preassessment activity	Preassessment graphic organizer* Establish clear rules	Gum, fidgets, putty, adapted pencils, "Handwriting Without Tears" paper for some students, picture prompts, rules written down, projector, laptop	Teacher leads Teacher assistant and paraeducator assist in scribing/writing for some students
2. Class brainstorming: What does "reducing" really mean?	Preformed Prezi presentation* on reducing		Student/paraeducator clicking and typing student ideas onto the Prezi presenta-tion
3. Reducing concept games and activities: What is being reduced? What is the effect?	Rules on board using both visuals and words		Related service providers can float to make sure rules are executed
4. Wrapup/postassessment: What did the students retain? How do they understand this concept as it relates to their personal impact on the environment and issues facing the world today?			Teacher leads

8. Review Notes & Suggestions: As the team reviews the draft lesson plan, note additional suggestions or improvements for the final draft.

Utilize a self-regulation scale to help students self-monitor and remain engaged.
Form groups with one student in each group capable of facilitating the brainstorming process.
Utilize an "island hopping" format. Each staff member runs a group and the students move from group to group.

9. School Documentation & Protocols: The team notes any mandated or IEP-driven goals and related services that might be addressed or satisfied by the lesson plan.

Send copy of final lesson plan to IEP lead/homeroom teacher. Provide copy of lesson plan to a family as basis of meeting during parent-teacher conference.

Name: ______
Date: ______
Class/Teacher: ______
Unit: ______

Lesson Plan a la Carte
TEAM Planning Step 3

TEAM Lesson Plan

**Each person in the classroom receives a double-sided copy of this plan.*

INTEGRATED LESSON PLAN — **Date of Implementation:**

1. Name & Brief Description of the Lesson:
Preassessment and ntroduction to the concept of reducing as it relates to students' personal responsibility to the environments around them.

2. Learning Objective(s):
Define reduction

Demonstrate understanding of reduction

Assess students' current understanding of the concept of reduction both outside and within the context of environmental awareness

3. Therapeutic Target Areas:
Concept formation

Personal relevance

Inattention/self-monitoring

4. Implementation

Activity	Strategies for Implementation	Supporting Materials	Lead & Team Supports
1. Quick gauge of everyone's regulatory level followed by preassessment activity	Preassessment graphic organizer* Establish clear rules	Gum, fidgets, putty, adapted pencils, "Handwriting Without Tears" paper for some students, picture prompts, rules written down, projector, laptop	Teacher leads Teacher assistant and paraeducator assist in scribing/writing for some students
2. Class brainstorming: What does "reducing" really mean?	Preformed Prezi presentation* on reducing Each student will have a clearly defined role within the small group (leader, scribe, reporter, etc.)		Student/paraeducator clicking and typing student ideas onto the Prezi presentation
3. Reducing concept games and activities: What is being reduced? What is the effect?	Rules on board using both visuals and words		Related service providers lead small groups while teacher and teacher assistant can float among students to make sure rules are executed

6. ASSESSMENT **Date:**

Rate the Lesson
On a scale of 1 to 5, rate how you feel the lesson generally went.
1 2 3 4 (5) — poorly, okay, very well

Notes:
The students were far more engaged in this lesson than they typically are.

Learning Objectives & Therapeutic Targets
Were the Learning Objectives satisfied?
☐ no ☐ partially ☑ yes

Were the Therapeutic Target Areas addressed?
☐ no ☐ partially ☑ yes

Notes:
As the teacher, I feel that my learning objectives were met.

Considerations for Planning
Were the Considerations for Planning successfully considered or implemented?
☐ no ☐ partially ☑ yes

Notes:
In the future, it would be a good idea to take more time setting up the technology in advance, as we couldn't get the computer program to function properly.

Name: ______
Date: ______
Class/Teacher: ______
Unit: ______

Lesson Plan a la Carte
TEAM Planning Step 3

TEAM Lesson Plan Cont.

Implementation Cont.

Activity	Strategies for Implementation	Supporting Materials	Lead & Team Supports
4. Wrapup/ postassessment: What did the students retain? How do they understand this concept as it relates to their personal impact on the environment?			Teacher leads

5. School Documentation & Protocols

Send copy of final lesson plan to IEP lead/homeroom teacher. Provide copy of lesson plan to family as basis of meeting during parent/teacher conference.

ASSESSMENT Cont.

Staff Roles
Were staff roles during implementation clear & successfully executed?
☐ no ☐ partially ☑ yes

Notes:
The related services providers helped keep the students in the lesson and without interrupting the flow.

Obstacles to Learning
Revisit the obstacles to learning that were identified by the team during the brainstorming session. Were the obstacles addressed by the lesson plan?
☐ no ☐ partially ☑ yes

Notes:
According to my post-assessment, the students understood and retained the information.

Documentation
Will you use this lesson plan as evidence for documenting IEP fidelity, IEP goals, SDI, RTI or other mandates/protocols? ☐ no ☑ yes

Notes:
Sent copy of lesson plan, along with assessment results, to main office to be filed with other integrated lessons for future review and use.

SOLO Lesson Plan Examples

Name: ____________________
Date: ____________________
Class/Teacher: ____________________
Unit: ____________________

Lesson Plan a la Carte
SOLO Planning Step 1

SOLO Draft Lesson Plan

Lesson Author: | **Date of Lesson Implementation:**

1. Name & Brief Description of the Lesson:

7th-grade science lab: the germination of seeds; experiment setup

2. Learning Objective(s):
Students will learn to follow lab directions for setting up germination experiment. Students will draft designs for data tables to demonstrate data collection over time (3-week period), with at least 2 quantitative variables to be documented in the data tables. Students will understand and demonstrate the characteristics of qualitative and quantitative data and show examples in their data tables.

3. Obstacles to Learning: List specific problems in the classroom that might pose obstacles to learning.

Even though her individual class work is good, Mary does poorly in labs when she has to collaborate with fellow students. She blurts out inappropriate remarks, interrupting class and other students.

4. Considerations for Planning: Turn to the Menu of Considerations for Planning. List any relevant items the team should do or keep in mind during implementation of the lesson so as to address the obstacles to learning in #3.

* Provide an incentive or motivating experience
* Provide supports for group work
* Reduce sensory triggers in the environment

5. Implementation Strategies: For each item you listed as a Consideration for Planning, provide details on how you will integrate these considerations into the lesson plan.

* Delegate construction of data tables to Mary as a task in her group; appeal to her strength/interest in tabulation, lists, and data
* Develop a list of scripts for "making suggestions" to a team member
* Assign Mary a screening role for lab materials. Ask her to collect data on dangers, sensory qualities, etc. Then present a brief overview to the class

6. Supporting Materials: If implementation of the lesson will require supporting materials, list them here. Supporting materials might include emotion charts, graphic organizers, fidgets, Power Cards, etc.

Seed germination kits (seeds, paper towel, jars, plastic baggies, soil, paper cups, colored light bulbs); scripts for "making suggestions" to a team member; descriptions of lab roles and responsibilities

Name: ____________________
Date: ____________________
Class/Teacher: ____________________
Unit: ____________________

Lesson Plan a la Carte
SOLO Planning Step 2

SOLO Lesson Plan

**Each staff in the classroom receives a double-sided copy of this plan.*

INTEGRATED LESSON PLAN **Date of Implementation:**

1. Name & Brief Description of the Lesson:
Setting up a seed germination lab for observation and data collection. Students will work in groups of 2, taking on specific lab roles: (1) data collection design and (2) lab setup, with sensory accommodations and supports for successful group work.

2. Learning Objective(s):
Students will learn to follow lab directions for setting up germination and observation experiments. Students will learn how to cooperate and make suggestions to one another in a lab setting. Students will draft designs for data tables that show data collection over 3-week period, with at least 3 variables (temperature, light, soil, location, etc.). Students will learn the characteristics of qualitative and quantitative data and show examples in their data tables. Students will work within the lab roles they have been assigned.

3. Implementation

Activity	Strategies for Implementation	Supporting Materials	Lead
Ask Mary to review lab materials during opening minutes of class Assign groups of 2 to lab stations	Provide supports for group work; provide an incentive or motivating experience; reduce sensory triggers in the environment	Kits include lab materials, plus descriptions of lab roles and responsibilities and scripts for "making suggestions" Cue Mary that she will be data designer in her lab group	Teacher Teacher aide (while teacher is working with Mary) Teacher aide passes out kits while teacher provides verbal overview

5. ASSESSMENT **Date:**

Rate the Lesson
On a scale of 1 to 5, rate how you feel the lesson generally went.
1 poorly 2 3 okay 4 (5) very well
Notes:
Mary responded very well to knowing her assigned role in the lab team. Written instructions helped her know her responsibilities and seemed to reduce stress. Also, the entire class benefited from this structure.

Learning Objectives
Were the Learning Objectives satisfied?
☐ no ☐ partially ☑ yes
Notes:
All learning objectives were met for Mary and for the class in general. Each team completed lab setup and designed data tables, working well within their assigned lab roles. Many teams made use of the scripts for "making suggestions." Mary used the scripts several times throughout the lesson.

Considerations for Planning
Were the Considerations for Planning successfully considered or implemented?
☐ no ☐ partially ☑ yes
Notes:
In the future, it would be a good idea to take more time with Mary on preteaching in order to make her feel more comfortable and able to process the material to be covered.

Name: ____________
Date: ____________
Class/Teacher: ____________
Unit: ____________

Lesson Plan a la Carte
SOLO Planning Step 2

SOLO Lesson Plan Cont.

Implementation Cont.

Activity	Strategies for Implementation	Supporting Materials	Lead & Team Supports
Distribute lab kits and provide overview of lab expectations, scripts for "making suggestions", and review of qualitative and quantitative data and variables			Teacher assists in materials overview, as needed
Mary presents on lab materials			Teacher and teacher assistant work with groups to ensure all aspects of integrated lesson plan are being covered
Students complete lab setup and data design according to their roles using provided scripts as needed			Teacher assistant offers Mary additional support in using scripts, if needed

4. School Documentation & Protocols

Send copy of final lesson plan with completed assessment to Mary's IEP lead/homeroom teacher. Provide copy of lesson plan to family as basis of meeting during parent-teacher conference.

ASSESSMENT Cont.

Staff Roles
Were staff roles during implementation clear & successfully executed?
☐ no ☐ partially ☑ yes
Notes:
The teacher assistant was more involved with students than in the past. She stepped in as planned, and I was able to delegate responsibility, particularly so that I could offer Mary 1:1 support in the opening minutes of the period.

Obstacles to Learning
Revisit the obstacles to learning that you identified your draft. Were the obstacles addressed by the lesson plan?
☐ no ☐ partially ☑ yes
Notes:
I have never seen Mary this integrated into class. She worked well with her partner and made no inappropriate remarks or comments that interrupted class. The overall plan helped the entire class to be more organized and work well in pairs.

Documentation
Will you use this lesson plan as evidence for documenting IEP fidelity, IEP goals, SDI, RTI or other mandates/protocols? ☐ no ☑ yes
Notes:
Sent copy of lesson plan, along with assessment results, to Mary's homeroom/IEP teacher. Parent-teacher conference scheduled for 11/17/2010.

REFERENCES

Aspy, R., & Grossman, B. G. (2012). *The Ziggurat Model: A framework for designing comprehensive interventions for high-functioning individuals with autism spectrum disorders. Release 2.0.* Shawnee Mission, KS: AAPC Publishing.

Case-Smith, J., & Holland, T. (2009). Making decisions about service delivery in early childhood programs. *Language, Speech, and Hearing Services in Schools, 40,* 416-423.

Endow, J. (2010). *Practical solutions for stabilizing students with classic autism to be ready to learn: Getting to go.* Shawnee Mission, KS: AAPC Publishing.

Heasley, S. (2010, August 16). Special education students bear brunt of suspensions. *Disability Scoop;* http://www.disabilityscoop.com/2010/08/16/texas-discipline/9777/

Henry, S. A., & Myles, B. S. (2007). *The Comprehensive Autism Planning Systems (CAPS) for individuals with Asperger Syndrome, autism and related disabilities: Integrating best practices throughout the student's day.* Shawnee Mission, KS: AAPC Publishing.

McIntosh, K., et al. (2008, October). Relationships between academics and problem behavior in the transition from middle school to high school. *Journal of Positive Behavior Interventions, 10*(4), 243-255.

Myles, B. S., Cook, T., Miller, N. E., Rinner, L., & Robbins, L. (2000). *Asperger Syndrome and sensory issues.* Shawnee Mission, KS: AAPC Publishing.

Murawski, W. W. (2010). *Collaborative teaching in elementary schools: Making the co-teaching marriage work!* Thousand Oaks, CA: Corwin.

APPENDIX

Appendix A: Overview of the Ziggurat Model and the Comprehensive Autism Planning System (CAPS)

Appendix B: Menus

 1. Therapeutic Menus

 2. Considerations for Planning Menus

Appendix C: Templates

TEAM Template Series

SOLO Template Series

Appendix A

Overview of the Ziggurat Model and the Comprehensive Autism Planning System (CAPS)

Recognized as the gold standard in comprehensive planning, the Ziggurat Model and the Comprehensive Autism Planning System (CAPS) provide a unique *process* and *framework* for designing and implementing comprehensive interventions for individuals of all ages with autism spectrum disorders (ASD). The models can be used alone or together. Each is designed to be completed by educational teams, including parents.

The Ziggurat Model

The Ziggurat Model is designed to address true needs or underlying deficits that result in social, emotional, and behavioral concerns. The model begins with an assessment of the individual's underlying needs and characteristics – a key component of the Ziggurat Model.

To that end, the Ziggurat Model includes the Underlying Characteristics Checklist (UCC), which provides a snapshot of how ASD is expressed for an individual. Three forms of this instrument exist – the UCC-HF for individuals with high-functioning autism, the UCC-CL for individuals with a classic presentation of autism, and the UCC-EI for early intervention. UCC items address the following characteristics validated by research: (a) social, (b) restricted behaviors/interests, (c) communication, (d) sensory differences, (e) cognitive differences, (f) motor differences, (g) emotional vulnerability and (h) known medical and other biological factors. An instrument designed to identify student strengths, the Individual Strengths and Skills Inventory (ISSI) follows the same format.

UCC-CL
UNDERLYING CHARACTERISTICS CHECKLIST-CLASSIC
Ruth Aspy, Ph.D., and Barry G. Grossman, Ph.D.

NAME: ______ DATE: ______ COMPLETED BY: ______
FOLLOW-UP DATE: ______ COMPLETED BY: ______

INSTRUCTIONS FOR COMPLETING INITIAL ASSESSMENT:
The UCC may be completed by an individual; however, the perspective of others who know and/or work with the person of focus is beneficial. Working as a team is optimal. Additionally, the team may include the individual who is the focus of the UCC as developmentally appropriate.

Each item describes behaviors or characteristics that may be exhibited by individuals with autism spectrum disorders. Please place a check beside ALL items that currently apply to the individual. Use the *Notes* column to describe the behavior and characteristics in more detail, provide specific examples, or indicate frequency, settings, etc.

Projected **Follow-Up** date: ______

Area	Item	✓	Notes	Follow-Up
SOCIAL	1. Has difficulty recognizing the feelings and thoughts of others (mindblindness)	✓	• *Often does not appear to recognize or respond when others cry* • *At other times, responses are inappropriate – laughs when others cry*	
	2. Uses poor eye contact or fails to orient to others			
	3. Shows little interest in or response to praise	✓	• *Acts as if he does not hear you* • *Does not do a given activity more even after being praised*	

INSTRUCTIONS FOR FOLLOW-UP ASSESSMENT:
Review checked and unchecked items. Use the *Notes* column to add further descriptors or to indicate changes. If item no longer applies, strike through the check and explain changes in the Follow-Up column, as illustrated below.

Area	Item	✓	Notes	Follow-Up
SOCIAL	1. Has difficulty recognizing the feelings and thoughts of others (mindblindness)	✓	• *Often does not appear to recognize or respond when others cry* • *At other times, responses are inappropriate – laughs when others cry*	• *Able to identify the feelings demonstrated in video scenarios and written stories*
	2. Uses poor eye contact or fails to orient to others			
	3. Shows little interest in or response to praise	✓ (struck)	• *Acts as if he does not hear you* • *Does not do a given activity more even after being praised*	• *Says, "Thank you" and smiles (sometimes with prompting)*

UCC-HF
UNDERLYING CHARACTERISTICS CHECKLIST-HIGH FUNCTIONING
Ruth Aspy, Ph.D., and Barry G. Grossman, Ph.D.

NAME: ______ DATE: ______ COMPLETED BY: ______
FOLLOW-UP DATE: ______ COMPLETED BY: ______

INSTRUCTIONS FOR COMPLETING INITIAL ASSESSMENT:
The UCC may be completed by an individual; however, the perspective of others who know and/or work with the person of focus is beneficial. Working as a team is optimal. Additionally, the team may include the individual who is the focus of the UCC as developmentally appropriate.

Each item describes behaviors or characteristics that may be exhibited by individuals with autism spectrum disorders. Please place a check beside ALL items that currently apply to the individual. Use the *Notes* column to describe the behavior and characteristics in more detail, provide specific examples, or indicate frequency, settings, etc.

Projected **Follow-up** date: ______

Area	Item	✓	Notes	Follow-Up
SOCIAL	1. Has difficulty recognizing the feelings and thoughts of others (mindblindness)	✓	• *Does not recognize when classmates tease or "set her up"* • *After being corrected at home, she repetitively asks her parents if they are still angry* • *In role plays, she can accurately identify the feelings of others 4 out of 10 times*	
	2. Uses poor eye contact			
	3. Has difficulty maintaining personal space, physically intrudes on others	✓	• *Sniffs peers' hair*	

INSTRUCTIONS FOR FOLLOW-UP ASSESSMENT:
Review checked and unchecked items. Use the *Notes* column to add further descriptors or to indicate changes. If item no longer applies, strike through the check and explain changes in the Follow-up column, as illustrated below.

Area	Item	✓	Notes	Follow-Up
SOCIAL	1. Has difficulty recognizing the feelings and thoughts of others (mindblindness)	✓	• *Does not recognize when classmates tease or "set her up"* • *After being corrected at home, she repetitively asks her parents if they are still angry* • *In role plays, she can accurately identify the feelings of others 4 out of 10 times*	• *Accurately reported that she was being teased last week* • *In role plays, she can now accurately identify others' feelings 6 out of 10 times*
	2. Uses poor eye contact			
	3. Has difficulty maintaining personal space, physically intrudes on others	✓ (struck)	• *Sniffs peers' hair*	• *No longer sniffs others. Follows rules for respecting personal space of others*

The Intervention Ziggurat contains five levels (see below) derived from research on ASD. Starting with the foundation level – Sensory Differences and Biological Needs – each level represents an area that must be addressed in order for an intervention plan to be comprehensive. Interventions at each level are selected to address the student's true needs (identified with the UCC) to ensure that "the autism" is addressed. Thus, interventions are meaningful – meeting underlying needs instead of masking them.

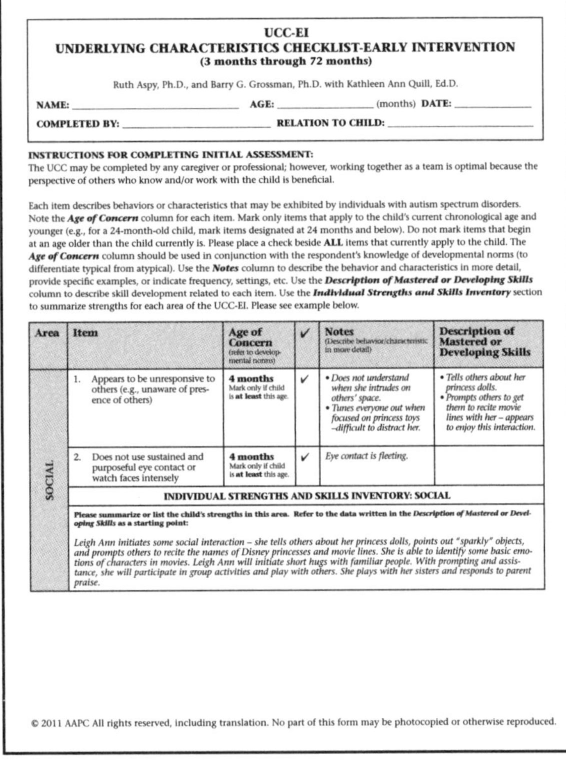

UCC-EI
UNDERLYING CHARACTERISTICS CHECKLIST-EARLY INTERVENTION
(3 months through 72 months)

Ruth Aspy, Ph.D., and Barry G. Grossman, Ph.D. with Kathleen Ann Quill, Ed.D.

NAME: ______ **AGE:** ______ (months) **DATE:** ______

COMPLETED BY: ______ **RELATION TO CHILD:** ______

INSTRUCTIONS FOR COMPLETING INITIAL ASSESSMENT:
The UCC may be completed by any caregiver or professional; however, working together as a team is optimal because the perspective of others who know and/or work with the child is beneficial.

Each item describes behaviors or characteristics that may be exhibited by individuals with autism spectrum disorders. Note the ***Age of Concern*** column for each item. Mark only items that apply to the child's current chronological age and younger (e.g., for a 24-month-old child, mark items designated at 24 months and below). Do not mark items that begin at an age older than the child currently is. Please place a check beside **ALL** items that currently apply to the child. The ***Age of Concern*** column should be used in conjunction with the respondent's knowledge of developmental norms (to differentiate typical from atypical). Use the ***Notes*** column to describe the behavior and characteristics in more detail, provide specific examples, or indicate frequency, settings, etc. Use the ***Description of Mastered or Developing Skills*** column to describe skill development related to each item. Use the ***Individual Strengths and Skills Inventory*** section to summarize strengths for each area of the UCC-EI. Please see example below.

Area	Item	Age of Concern (refer to developmental norms)	✓	Notes (Describe behavior/characteristic in more detail)	Description of Mastered or Developing Skills
SOCIAL	1. Appears to be unresponsive to others (e.g., unaware of presence of others)	**4 months** Mark only if child is **at least** this age.	✓	• *Does not understand when she intrudes on others' space.* • *Tunes everyone out when focused on princess toys –difficult to distract her.*	• *Tells others about her princess dolls.* • *Prompts others to get them to recite movie lines with her – appears to enjoy this interaction.*
	2. Does not use sustained and purposeful eye contact or watch faces intensely	**4 months** Mark only if child is **at least** this age.	✓	*Eye contact is fleeting.*	
	INDIVIDUAL STRENGTHS AND SKILLS INVENTORY: SOCIAL				
	Please summarize or list the child's strengths in this area. Refer to the data written in the *Description of Mastered or Developing Skills* as a starting point: *Leigh Ann initiates some social interaction – she tells others about her princess dolls, points out "sparkly" objects, and prompts others to recite the names of Disney princesses and movie lines. She is able to identify some basic emotions of characters in movies. Leigh Ann will initiate short hugs with familiar people. With prompting and assistance, she will participate in group activities and play with others. She plays with her sisters and responds to parent praise.*				

INTERVENTION ZIGGURAT

Skills to Teach
Address skill deficits

- Social
- Restricted patterns
- Communication
- Sensory
- Cognitive
- Motor
- Emotional

Task Demands
Remove obstacles

- Social
- Restricted patterns
- Communication
- Sensory
- Cognitive
- Motor
- Emotional

Structure and Visual/Tactile Supports

Create predictability

- Prepare for change
- Provide routine
- Walk through new activities

Use visual/tactile supports to hold information still

- Video
- Stories and cartoons
- Schedules and checklists
- Graphic/tactile organizers

Reinforcement

Provide reinforcement

- Contingent on expected behavior
- Frequent and consistent
- Self-selected
- Gradually decrease use

Provide range of reinforcers

- Concrete, activities, privileges
- Use restricted interests
- Pair social with tangible reinforcement

Sensory and Biological

Provide a sensory diet
Monitor and address environmental stressors:

- Sound, light, proximity/personal space, textures
- Movement needs

Monitor and address:

- Appetite/hunger
- Activity level (e.g., fatigue, hyper)
- Posture and movement
- Medical needs

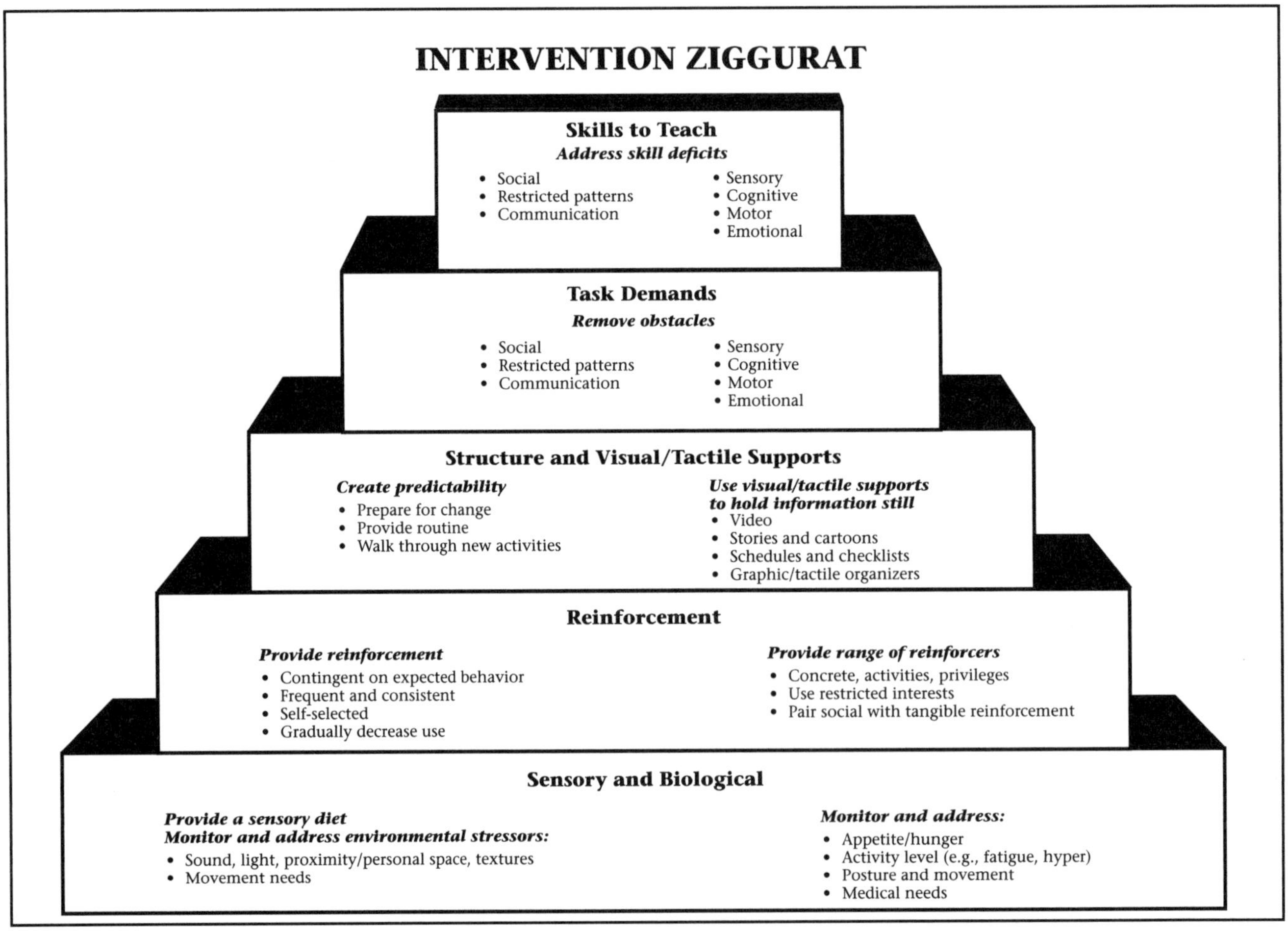

The Comprehensive Autism Planning System

The Comprehensive Autism Planning System (CAPS) is designed to provide an overview of a student's daily schedule by time and activity as well as the supports that are needed during each period. Following the development of the student's IEP, all educational professionals who work with the student develop the CAPS. The CAPS allows professionals and parents to answer the all-important question: What supports does the student need for each activity? The CAPS is a list of a student's daily tasks and activities, the times they occur, along with the delineation of supports needed for student success. In addition, the CAPS includes space for making notations about data collection and how skills are to be generalized to others settings.

Summary

The Ziggurat Model and the CAPS are valuable resources for public school professionals who must remain in compliance with federal and state guidelines. Specifically, recent trends in special education law emphasize the use of scientifically based research approaches. In addition, there is a strong push for incorporating positive behavioral interventions and supports (PBIS). The Ziggurat Model and CAPS are consistent with these practices. First, evidenced-based interventions are incorporated in the Ziggurat and the CAPS model. Both also emphasizes a proactive, positive approach by requiring reinforcement and antecedent-based interventions. Finally, the Ziggurat Model and CAPS promote collaboration and communication among parents and professionals.

Comprehensive Autism Planning System (CAPS)

Child/Student: ______________________________

Time	Activity	Targeted Skills to Teach	Structure/ Modifications	Reinforcement	Sensory Strategies	Communication/ Social Skills	Data Collection	Generalization Plan

APPENDIX B

Lesson Plan a la Carte

Therapeutic Menus

Considerations for Planning

(See also the enclosed CD)

Therapeutic Menus

The Therapeutic Menus are not comprehensive. They are meant to spur your thinking, particularly in the brainstorming process. Because some clinical descriptions not listed in the standard menus will inevitably arise once you begin using them, we have provided additional space for you or your team to add new items. We suggest that you build on these menus adding descriptions that recur in your particular setting.

Additionally, as you read through the items in any of the four Therapeutic Menus, you will note that descriptions from various categories might appear to apply. For instance, "understanding social rules" appears in both the Language and Communication and the Social and Emotional Menus. This flexibility is meant to prompt you to reflect on the obstacles to learning across the fullest range of descriptive categories possible.

With time, you'll find using the Therapeutic Menus becomes more than just an exercise. In fact, it is an important point in the planning process where clinical and educational perspectives are bridged and come to enrich each other. Once you have identified key clinical descriptions, both clinicians and teachers can focus on key issues (or therapeutic targets) as you write the lesson plan.

Therapeutic Menu #1

Language & Communication

Use this menu as a TEAM brainstorming tool. Identify possible clinical descriptions of obstacles to learning you see in the classroom. The menu is not comprehensive. Add more language and communication descriptions in the space provided, as needed.

Areas of Receptive Language, Memory, and Auditory Processing Difficulty

- ☐ Understanding and following verbal directions
- ☐ Concept formation
- ☐ Organization of verbally presented information
- ☐ Understanding social rules
- ☐ Sensitivity to noise
- ☐ Needing words or sentences repeated
- ☐ Hearing clearly in noisy environments
- ☐ Learning and remembering new material
- ☐ Remembering details immediately and some time after verbal presentation
- ☐ Remembering details immediately and some time after visual presentation
- ☐ Interprets words too literally
- ☐ Remembering a list or sequence
- ☐ Seems to ignore others when engrossed in a non-speaking activity
- ☐ Remembering faces
- ☐ Misses contextual cues
- ☐ ____________________
- ☐ ____________________
- ☐ ____________________

Areas of Expressive Language Difficulties

Language Formation

- ☐ Pragmatics: rules that govern language
- ☐ Semantics: rules that govern language content
- ☐ Syntax: formulation of grammatical sentences
- ☐ Morphology and phonology: rules that govern the formation and pronunciation of words, and recognizing similarities and differences (as in rhyming)
- ☐ ____________________

Speech

- ☐ Articulation
- ☐ Prosody and tone
- ☐ Volume: speaks louder or softer than necessary
- ☐ ____________________

Areas of Verbal and Nonverbal Reasoning Difficulty

Verbal Reasoning

- ☐ Comparing and contrasting
- ☐ Explaining social rules and everyday concerns
- ☐ Paraphrasing text
- ☐ ____________________

Nonverbal Reasoning

- ☐ Recognizing patterns
- ☐ Solving problems with visual information
- ☐ Organization of visual information
- ☐ Parts-to-whole thinking
- ☐ Problem-solving strategies
- ☐ Theory of mind: perspective shifting, understanding mental states of self and other
- ☐ ____________________

Therapeutic Menu #2

Attention & Executive Function

Use this menu as a TEAM brainstorming tool. Identify possible clinical descriptions of obstacles to learning you see in the classroom. The menu is not comprehensive. Add more attention and executive function descriptions in the space provided.

- ☐ Visual attention
- ☐ Auditory attention
- ☐ Inhibitory control/ impulsivity/ hyperactivity
- ☐ Cognitive set shifting: switching between different sets of rules depending on task
- ☐ Self-initiation of work
- ☐ Thinking flexibly
- ☐ Staying on track
- ☐ Working memory: ability to attend to and hold the information in mind, as well as mentally manipulate it
- ☐ Prioritizing
- ☐ Cognitive fluency: generating ideas quickly and systematically/ picking a topic
- ☐ Organizing work/ assignments/ belongings
- ☐ Breaking a project down into manageable units
- ☐ Sequencing steps to complete a task
- ☐ Self-monitoring: self-prompting, reviewing strategies, self-evaluation
- ☐ Time management: task analysis and time estimation
- ☐ Categorization
- ☐ Information-processing speed
- ☐ Rigid adherence to schedules and routines
- ☐ Managing transitions between subjects or topics
- ☐ Managing transitions between classes
- ☐ ______________________________
- ☐ ______________________________
- ☐ ______________________________
- ☐ ______________________________
- ☐ ______________________________
- ☐ ______________________________
- ☐ ______________________________

Therapeutic Menu #3

Social & Emotional

Use this menu as a TEAM brainstorming tool. Identify possible clinical descriptions of obstacles to learning you see in the classroom. The menu is not comprehensive. Add more social and emotional descriptions in the space provided.

Areas of Social Difficulty

- ☐ Reading nonverbal cues/ body language
- ☐ Compulsivity
- ☐ Interrupts conversations
- ☐ Concrete and inflexible in social situations
- ☐ Making small talk
- ☐ Initiating conversations
- ☐ Being proactive in making friends
- ☐ Reading facial expressions
- ☐ Differentiating between humor and sarcasm
- ☐ Responds negatively to criticism
- ☐ Easily persuaded
- ☐ Defensive in social situations
- ☐ Disorganized and inattentive
- ☐ Seeing the consequences of actions
- ☐ Being oriented in time and space
- ☐ Managing money
- ☐ Misses opportunities to demonstrate strengths
- ☐ Poor eye contact
- ☐ Maintaining personal space
- ☐ Lacks tact or appears rude
- ☐ Understanding jokes
- ☐ Asks repetitive questions
- ☐ Accepting roles in group interactions
- ☐ Working within a small group
- ☐ Initiating and responding to social greetings
- ☐ Asking for help
- ☐ ____________________
- ☐ ____________________
- ☐ ____________________

Areas of Emotional Difficulty

- ☐ Describing feelings of frustration or anger
- ☐ Undeveloped coping skills
- ☐ Low self-esteem
- ☐ Anxious to speak but trouble following conversations
- ☐ Being able to handle setbacks
- ☐ Responds negatively to criticism
- ☐ Recognizing emotions of self and other
- ☐ Vulnerability to depression due to past failures and victimization
- ☐ Uncomfortable trying new things
- ☐ Appropriate fear response
- ☐ Rage reactions
- ☐ Injures self
- ☐ Stress management
- ☐ Self-soothing
- ☐ ____________________
- ☐ ____________________

Therapeutic Menu #4

Sensory & Regulatory

Use this menu as a TEAM brainstorming tool. Identify possible clinical descriptions of obstacles to learning you see in the classroom. The menu is not comprehensive. Add more sensory and regulatory descriptions as the team identifies them.

Areas of Visual Processing Difficulty

Spatial Relationships

- ☐ Ability to perceive words and numbers as separate units
- ☐ Directionality problems
- ☐ Confusion of similarly shaped letters, such as b/d or p/q
- ☐ ______________________________

Visual Discrimination

- ☐ Ability to identify differences between objects
- ☐ Ability to recognize an object as distinct from its surrounding environment
- ☐ Ability to use visually presented material in a productive way
- ☐ ______________________________

Visual Closure

- ☐ Ability to identify or recognize a symbol or object when the entire object is not visible
- ☐ ______________________________

Whole/Part relationships

- ☐ Perceiving or integrating the relationship between an object (or symbol) in its entirety and the component parts that make it up
- ☐ ______________________________

Areas of Motor Coordination

Gross Motor

- ☐ Bilateral integration: ability to use two sides of the body together
- ☐ Gravitational insecurity: an emotional or fear reaction that is out of proportion to the actual threat regarding position in space
- ☐ Balance
- ☐ Intolerance or aversive response to movement
- ☐ Motor planning: producing projected action sequences
- ☐ Strength and postural tone/stability issues
- ☐ Kinesthesia: awareness of body position in space
- ☐ ______________________________

Fine Motor

- ☐ Grasp
- ☐ Manipulation: unilateral and/or bimanual
- ☐ Graphomotor
- ☐ Tactile discrimination
- ☐ ______________________________

Other Areas of Sensory Processing

Sensory Over-Responsivity or Under-Responsivity

- ☐ Having a high or low threshold for touch, taste, smell, hearing, vision, body movement (proprioception), and/or head position and movement in space (vestibular)
- ☐ ______________________________

Sensory Modulation

- ☐ Ability to down-regulate or up-regulate to maintain an optimal balance between attending to relevant stimuli and screening out unnecessary input
- ☐ May seek stimuli to point of distraction or self-injury
- ☐ May avoid stimuli to point of non-participation in activity
- ☐ ______________________________

Considerations for Planning Menus

The Considerations for Planning Menus are not meant to be comprehensive. If the strategies listed here aren't the precise solution for your particular lesson plan and student(s), use them as a guide to assist you in discovering your own solutions and strategies. Additional space is provided in the menus to add more considerations and strategies that recur in your setting or that you or your team discover and develop along the way.

Note: For strategies marked with an asterisk (*), more information may be found on pages 79-81.

Considerations for Planning

Use the menus below as you write the DRAFT Integrated Lesson Plan in TEAM or SOLO planning. Identify relevant environmental, instructional, or additional considerations to keep in mind when the lesson plan is implemented. Some examples of strategies for implementation are offered below. The Considerations for Planning Menus and the strategy examples are not comprehensive; they are meant as a guide for developing strategies specific to your students and classroom as you write the DRAFT Integrated Lesson Plan. The team may add more considerations and strategies for implementation to the menus below where space is provided, creating a library of options that school personnel can tap into.

1. **Considerations for the Learning Environment**	1. **Implementation Strategies: Learning Environment**
• Eliminate distractions and consider where students' focus is drawn	• Close doors, remove distracting posters or images from classroom, avoid use of air fresheners or perfume, reduce or eliminate the use of fluorescent lighting
• Vary learning positions	• Offer seating and positioning alternatives (e.g., therapy ball, sitting on floor, lying down, sitting backwards on chair, standing)
• Create space to regulate arousal (up-regulate* or down-regulate*)	• Offer short breaks in a calm, quiet environment, a quiet room, or the hallway; alternatively a place to up-regulate or get re-energized, like a place to take a walk or jump on a trampoline)
• Reduce overstimulation but maximize social integration	• Arrange student seating
• Facilitate greater autonomy	• Ensure that learning spaces are organized and visually labeled

2a. Considerations for Instructional Enhancements Presentation	2a. Implementation Strategies Presentation
• Make task instructions accessible	• Simplify verbal and written instructions, reinforce instructions (once is not enough!), reduce number of steps in command, make instructional language concrete/less abstract
• Make verbal presentation accessible	• Use concrete language for more novel material (then work towards abstract), slow rate of presentation, modulate tone and volume, increase contrast and intensity of presentation as material becomes more familiar
• Make visual presentation accessible	• Enlarge print for reading, handouts, worksheets, and other materials; utilize three-dimensional material/models, then add two-dimensional and dynamic images/models
• Make expectations explicit in writing or visually	• Write expectations on white-board or post on walls

2b. Considerations for Instructional Enhancements Content	2b. Implementation Strategies Content
• Prime students for lessons • Preteach • Activate prior knowledge • Provide repetition, familiarity, and consistency • Use "real-life" situations to teach • Make the context of each part of the lesson explicit • Check students' interpretations of events for accuracy • Include an individual or group self-evaluation	• Provide agendas for activities in today's class • Pre-assign group discussion questions as homework • Review what happened in previous class • Use self-evaluation statements (e.g., One thing I learned from this activity is ________.)

2c. Considerations for Instructional Enhancements Format	2c. Implementation Strategies Format
• Reduce length of assignments or quantity of work without sacrificing depth	• Assign every other question for in-class assignments or homework
• Embed lessons with contingency statements	• Use statements such as, "When we finish reading this, it will be time for snack"
• "Chunk" or break lessons and activities into discrete steps	• Remember the rule of thumb: Make what seems to take one step into an activity that takes three steps
• Provide an incentive or motivating experience	• Incorporate a student's special interest. For example, you could use the Power Cards* system developed by Elisa Gagnon
• Embed review of material regularly throughout lesson	• Utilize a 10:2 approach*, 10 minutes of instruction and 2 minutes of review
• Embed regular breaks throughout lesson	• Give brief movement breaks* or "shake out" your body exercises
• Prepare students for content or activity transitions	• Provide a visual outline/agenda* for each class

3. **Considerations for Further Communication & Language Enhancements**	3. **Implementation Strategies: Communication & Language**
• Support students in expressing choices, wants, and needs	• Use visual cards
• Underscore verbal communication with nonverbal input	• Emphasize gestures while speaking, use sign language
• Ensure consistent access to communication and language support	• Provide a designated reader and/or scribe
• Identify what is on/off topic	• Cue students to do "check-ins" on their comments during class discussions or group activities
• Develop sight word mastery	• Offer weekly vocabulary or a "word of the day"
• Build in specific opportunities to practice skills that develop vocabulary, rhyming, segmenting, and blending words	• Play word game activities, music with lyrics, or team games involving vocabulary
• Use a developmental approach to writing	• Start with sentence structure, then move to paragraph structure, then to transitioning to new ideas within a paragraph, and finally to elaborating on a main idea
• Foster reciprocity in communication	• Establish eye contact prior to giving essential instructions or new material
• Consistently monitor comprehension	• Establish "check-in" routines for students spaced regularly through the class hour, use special language or prompts to elicit review of what was learned
• Use a developmental approach to comprehension	• Start by teaching to describe, then to sequence, then to summarize, and finally full comprehension of the main idea
• Teach discrimination between facts and opinion	• Use humorous scripts or cartoons; ask students to create their own
• Teach how to make predictions	• Have students fill in missing words or complete sentences
• Elicit active language to questions	

4. **Considerations for Further Attention & Executive Function Enhancements**	4. **Implementation Strategies: Attention & Executive Function**
• Develop predictable and consistent routines	• Post schedules, go over changes in routine in advance, create a binder or "cookbook" of steps for common routines or assignments, keep assignments folders in specific and consistent locations
• Develop effective visual aids	• Use visual aids in schedules, color code, use pictures of classes or teachers, simplify structure and amount of material contained on worksheets, divide paper into large and discrete sections (especially for math problems), provide work samples to promote independence
• Develop time management skills	• Use task analysis,* practice time estimation, use time lines, use to-do lists, and work on prioritizing
• Develop attentional capacity	• Teach verbal mediation or "self-talk"* for attention and problem solving, have students verbalize a plan or approach to a task, build frequent "check-ins" into assignments based on intermediate deadlines, develop checklists for independent work
• Develop organizational capacity	• Establish daily routines for school organization with a written version in a notebook, hold a "housekeeping" period to allow students to get organized, provide an extra set of textbooks for home use, work with students to identify individual strategies they've found helpful

5. Considerations for Further Social & Emotional Enhancements	5. Implementation Strategies: Social & Emotional
• Facilitate peer relationships that provide opportunities for mentorship and modeling	• Establish a "partner classroom" with a general ed classroom
• Provide supports for team or group work	• Use scripting, delineating, and modeling of roles
• Vary group size according to need	• Use larger group games for teambuilding fun, paired work for collaboration (limit academic work done in groups of 3 or 4)
• Generalize modifications and teaching strategies for the entire class	• Remember that most strategies are beneficial to the entire class
• Develop a set of discreet cues for teacher-student communication	• Use cards or hand signals; for emergency movement breaks* or redirection, send student on an errand
• Foster a cooperative learning environment	• Cue students to create a list of activities, attitudes, or behaviors that foster cooperation and post in classroom
• Establish individual relationships with students	• Encourage ongoing dialogue with student through a regular journal or alternative form of regular communication
• Assign social roles	• Assign roles as greeters, conflict resolvers, helpers, etc.
• Foster interdependence whenever possible	• Play round-robin games, pass the statement around the circle: "how you helped me this week"
• Encourage self-monitoring skills, build emotional vocabulary	• Develop and teach use of emotional thermometer* with brief, regular check-ins (try the Incredible 5-Point Scale* developed by Kari Dunn Buron and Mitzi Curtis)
• Establish a safe place to cool down	• Create a "safe room" or safe person/home base* person
• Provide positive behavioral support	• Use reinforcement schedules, labeled praise, effective commands, prompting, selective and active ignoring, and teach and involve students in goal-setting process

6. **Considerations for Further Sensory & Regulatory Enhancements**	6. **Implementation Strategies: Sensory & Regulatory**
• Reduce sensory triggers in the environment	• Screen a task or activity for sensory characteristics that may present as overstimulating, decrease all sensory aspects* of lessons for new material
• Provide sensory strategies for self-regulation* and self-awareness	• Develop a sensory schedule* for a class or individuals within a class (e.g. Brain Gym® exercises developed by Paul and Gail Dennison, "heavy work"* breaks, snacks), provide a sensory "tool chest"* for classes (may include gum, fidgets, weighted vests, slant board, etc.)
• Encourage self-direction in self-regulation*	• Help student choose and develop guidelines for self-initiated breaks, send student on a "heavy work"* errand to down-regulate* (or reduce over-stimulation) and recover focus

7. **Considerations for Special Materials**	7. **Implementation Strategies: Special Materials**
• Remove obstacles to learning or enhance the learning environment through use of special materials	• Provide oral motor inputs* (gum, "chewelry,"* etc.) • Use timers (with and without auditory cues) • Use reading "window" (index card or commercially purchased) • Provide special paper (dark lined, raised line, etc.) • Use pastel paper instead of white for handouts (to accommodate visual processing) • Make manipulatives available (to increase attention and reduce anxiety) • Use odorless markers for white-board • Provide ear plugs or noise-canceling headphones • Provide technology (laptops for keyboarding skills, writing software, time management software, etc.) • Use an audio recorder to capture responses

Definitions and Sources for *Lesson Plan a la Carte*

The list below offers definitions and sources for foundational techniques and strategies commonly used to support students with a variety of special needs.

Items marked with an asterisk (*) are curricular modules developed by the Ohio Center for Autism and Low Incidence (OCALI), and available as free downloads at http://www.autisminternetmodules.org/index.php.

10:2 – 10 minutes of instruction, followed by 2 minutes of review

Chewlery – see the *Abilitations* catalog; available online or in print, www.abilitations.com

Down-Regulate – performing a sensory-based calming activity

Emotions Thermometer – a visual way to organize and monitor one's emotional levels; see also *Incredible 5-Point Scale*

Graphic Organizers – a method of organizing information visually, such as spider map, Venn diagram, describing wheel, etc.; see www.inspiration.com

Heavy Work – motor activities used to help increase attention and modulate emotion, such as carrying books, running an errand, etc; for more information visit http://www.sensory-processing-disorder.com/heavy-work-activities.html

*Home Base** – a person or place to provide sensory and/or emotional support when needed

*Incredible 5-Point Scale** – a visual method of organizing energy and emotion levels developed by Kari Dunn and Mitzi Beth Curtis; see www.aapcpublishing.net

Movement Breaks – breaks that can be scheduled and/or permitted when a student can utilize it for self-regulation

Oral Motor Inputs – students may require a crunchy food or an effective piece of *chewelry* (see above) to satisfy need for oral input; visit http://www.sensory-processing-disorder.com/oral-sensitivities.html

PECS – or Picture Exchange Communication System (Andrew Bondy, Ph.D., and Lori Frost, MS, CCC/SLP, Pyramid Educational Consultants) is a communication system that uses pictures, rather than words, to support individuals in communication; visit www.pecsusa.com

Emotions Thermometer

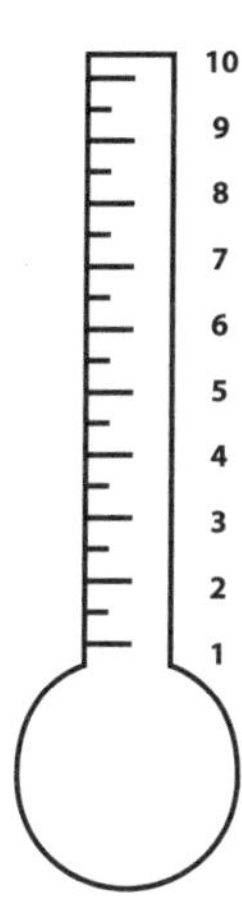

Graphic Organizer

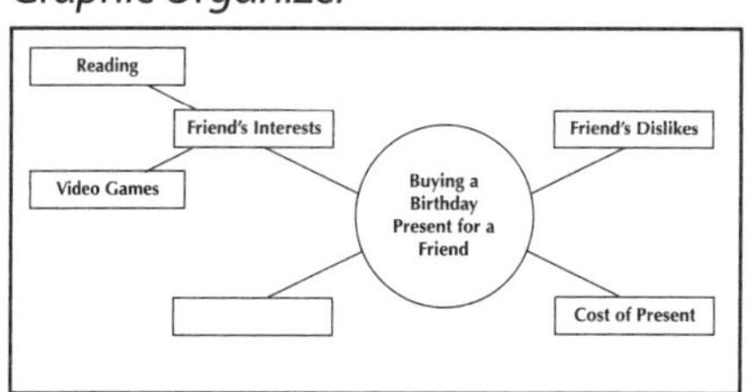

From *Big picture thinking: Using central coherence theory to support social skills*, A. Collucci, 2011. Shawnee Mission, KS: AAPC Publishing. Used with permission.

Sample 5-Point Scale

Level	Person, place or thing	Makes me feel like this:
5		This could make me lose control!!!!
4		This can *really* upset me.
3		This can make me feel nervous.
2		This sometimes bothers me.
1		This never bothers me.

From *A "5" could make me lose control!*, K. Dunn Buron, 2007, Shawnee Mission, KS: AAPC Publishing. Reprinted with permission.

*Power Cards** – using the student's special interest, a card is made with engaging and motivating visuals and text to provide specific instructions for behavioral, social, or academic tasks; see Gagnon, E. (2001). *Power Cards: Using Special Interests to Motivate Children and Youth with Asperger Syndrome and Autism*, www.aapcpublishing.net; see also http://autismspectrum.illinoisstate.edu/resources/factsheets/powercard.shtml

Power Card

Sam

Sam is a highly intelligent sixth-grade student with a diagnosis of Asperger Syndrome. Sam hopes one day to attend Harvard and often speaks of this plan to anyone willing to listen. But even though Sam is intelligent, he has developed few organizational strategies. Specifically, he doesn't ask questions about course requirements and therefore often fails to turn in assignments on time. The following scenario and POWER CARD were introduced to Sam by his mother to provide him with organizational strategies.

From *Power cards: Using special interests to motivate children and youth with Asperger Syndrome and Autism*, E. Gagnon, 2001. Shawnee Mission, KS: AAPC Publishing. Reprinted with permission.

1. Take class notes and write all assignments in a calendar.
2. Ask questions when you don't understand.
3. Break down assignments into small steps, assign deadlines for each step, and write all deadlines and assignment due dates in a calendar.

*Prezi Presentation** – web-based application and storytelling tool that uses a single canvas instead of traditional slides

*Self-Management** – using self-regulation strategies to control one's behavior; see *Self-Regulation*

Self-Regulation – the ability to independently regulate one's mood and/or behavior

Self-Talk – student talks to self (can also be silent/internal) as a means of remembering effective behaviors, techniques, or strategies to successfully navigate various situations

Sensory Aspects – elements of a situation or environment that may affect a student's ability to process sensory experiences

Sensory Differences – differences in how an individual processes sights, sounds, smells, touch, and the body's location or movement in space. A person with sensory challenges can experience hyper- and/or hyposensitivity within one or more of the sense systems; see also *ISA Sensory Scan™*

ISA Sensory Scan™ – a tool developed by Valerie Paradiz that supports individuals in examining specific environments for discomforts or triggers that may involve sensory sensitivities; see *The Integrated Self-Advocacy ISA™ Curriculum: A Program for Emerging Self-Advocates with Autism Spectrum and Other Conditions*; www.aapcpublishing.net

Sensory Schedule – a means of anticipating the students' arousal level at certain times of the day, during certain activities, or a tool for providing sensory breaks at regular/planned intervals

Sensory Tool Chest – various techniques (e.g., movement breaks) and materials (e.g., fidgets or ball chairs) used for sensory modulation

*Social Narratives** – texts written in words, and often supported by pictures, that offer an individual opportunity for review and practice for various social skills that will be needed in a specific situation or environment (e.g., going to a restaurant or visiting relatives). For example, see http://www.thewatsoninstitute.org/teacher-resources2.jsp?pageId=2161392240601226415747290

*Task Analysis** – breaking down what might seem to be "one task" into numerous small steps. This ensures understanding and completion of each small step, which in turn ensures successful completion of entire task

Up-Regulate – performing a sensory-based "alerting" activity

Visual Agenda or *Visual Schedules** – pictures, and sometimes words, used to show students the activities that will occur at specific times throughout the day

Wait Time – the amount of time provided to a student to answer a question

Visual Schedules

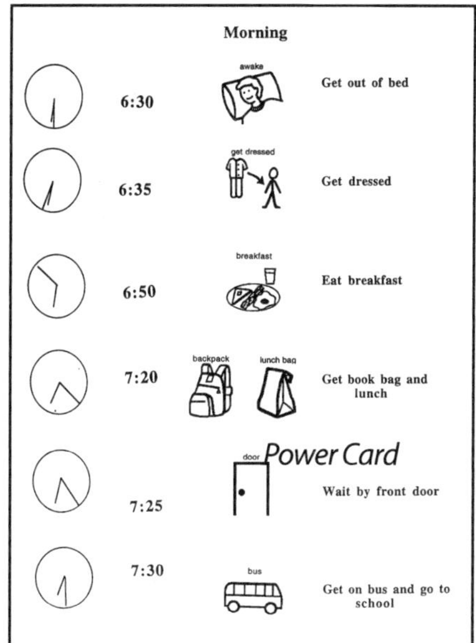

From *Making visual supports work in the home and community: Strategies for individuals with autism and Asperger Syndrome*, J. L. Savner & B.S. Myles, 2000. Shawnee Mission, KS: AAPC Publishing. Reprinted with permission.

APPENDIX C

Lesson Plan a la Carte

Planning Templates:

TEAM

- **TEAM Brainstorming**
- **TEAM Draft Lesson Plan**
- **TEAM Lesson Plan**

SOLO

- **SOLO Draft Lesson Plan**
- **SOLO Lesson Plan**

(See also the enclosed CD)

Name: ______________________
Date: ______________________
Class/Teacher: ______________________
Unit: ______________________

Lesson Plan a la Carte
TEAM Planning Step 1

TEAM Brainstorming

1 Introduce Learning Objective

The initiating teacher or therapist briefly presents the learning objective(s)

2 Identify Obstacles to Learning

A. Each team member lists specific problems in the classroom that might pose obstacles to learning.	**B.** Using the four Therapeutic Menus, team members identify possible clinical descriptions of the problems described in column A.
Obstacles to Learning	**Possible Clinical Descriptions**

3 Identify Therapeutic Target Areas & Brainstorm Integrated Lesson Ideas

A. Team members briefly present their answers from columns A and B above. Using this information, the team identifies the most relevant areas of difficulty to target with therapeutic intervention(s).	**B.** Next, the team brainstorms lesson ideas that integrate therapeutic interventions with learning objectives.
Areas to Target With Therapeutic Intervention(s)	**Integrated Lesson Ideas**

4 Name the Lesson & Choose Author(s)

The team considers the strengths and weaknesses of the lesson ideas and determines which should be implemented. Next, the team creates a name for the lesson and chooses the lesson plan author(s).

Lesson Name:	**Lesson Author(s):**
Lesson Draft Review Date:	**Date of Lesson Implementation:**

Name: ______________________
Date: ______________________
Class/Teacher: ______________________
Unit: ______________________

Lesson Plan a la Carte
TEAM Planning Step 2

TEAM Draft Lesson Plan

Lesson Author(s):	**Date of Lesson Implementation:**

1. Name & Brief Description of the Lesson:	
2. Learning Objective(s):	**3. Therapeutic Target Areas:**
4. Considerations for Planning: Turn to the Menu of Considerations for Planning and list any relevant items the team should do or keep in mind during implementation.	**5. Implementation Strategies:** For each item you listed as a Consideration for Planning, provide details on how you will integrate these considerations into the lesson plan.
6. Supporting Materials: If implementation of the lesson will require supporting materials, list them here. Supporting materials might include emotioncharts, graphic organizers, fidgets, Power Cards,* etc.	

Name: ______________________
Date: ______________________
Class/Teacher: ______________________
Unit: ______________________

Lesson Plan a la Carte
TEAM Planning Step 2

TEAM Draft Lesson Plan Cont.

7. Implementation: Divide the lesson into discrete activities, describing each step deliberately. Next to the activity description, list the specific implementation strategies and supporting materials the team will use, and clearly indicate who will take the lead in each step. Be certain that each staff member in the classroom has a defined role, including teachers, therapists, paraprofessionals, and assistants. Students need this clarity in order to be successful.

Activity	Strategies for Implementation	Supporting Materials	Lead & Team Supports

8. Review Notes & Suggestions: As the team reviews the draft lesson plan, note additional suggestions or improvements for the final draft.

9. School Documentation & Protocols: The team notes any mandated or IEP-driven goals and related services that might be addressed or satisfied by the lesson plan.

Name: ____________________
Date: ____________________
Class/Teacher: ____________________
Unit: ____________________

Lesson Plan a la Carte
TEAM Planning Step 3

TEAM Lesson Plan

**Each person in the classroom receives a double-sided copy of this plan.*

INTEGRATED LESSON PLAN	Date of Implementation:
1. Name & Brief Description of the Lesson:	
2. Learning Objective(s):	**3. Therapeutic Target Areas:**

4. Implementation

Activity	Strategies for Implementation	Supporting Materials	Lead & Team Supports

6. ASSESSMENT Date:

Rate the Lesson
On a scale of 1 to 5, rate how you feel the lesson generally went.
1 2 3 4 5
poorly okay very well
Notes:

Learning Objectives & Therapeutic Targets
Were the Learning Objectives satisfied?
☐ no ☐ partially ☐ yes
Were the Therapeutic Target Areas addressed?
☐ no ☐ partially ☐ yes
Notes:

Considerations for Planning
Were the Considerations for Planning successfully considered or implemented?
☐ no ☐ partially ☐ yes
Notes:

Name: ______________________
Date: ______________________
Class/Teacher: ______________________
Unit: ______________________

Lesson Plan a la Carte
TEAM Planning Step 3

TEAM Lesson Plan Cont.

Implementation Cont.

Activity	Strategies for Implementation	Supporting Materials	Lead & Team Supports

5. School Documentation & Protocols

ASSESSMENT Cont.

Staff Roles
Were staff roles during implementation clear & successfully executed?
☐ no ☐ partially ☐ yes
Notes:

Obstacles to Learning
Revisit the obstacles to learning that were identified by the team during the brainstorming session. Were the obstacles addressed by the lesson plan?
☐ no ☐ partially ☐ yes
Notes:

Documentation
Will you use this lesson plan as evidence for documenting IEP fidelity, IEP goals, SDI, RTI or other mandates/protocols? ☐ no ☐ yes
Notes:

Name: __________________
Date: __________________
Class/Teacher: __________________
Unit: __________________

Lesson Plan a la Carte
SOLO Planning Step 1

SOLO Draft Lesson Plan

Lesson Author:	**Date of Lesson Implementation:**

1. Name & Brief Description of the Lesson:	
2. Learning Objective(s):	**3. Obstacles to Learning:** List specific problems in the classroom that might pose obstacles to learning.
4. Considerations for Planning: Turn to the Menu of Considerations for Planning. List any relevant items the team should do or keep in mind during implementationof the lesson so as to address the obstacles to learning in #3.	**5. Implementation Strategies:** For each item you listed as a Consideration for Planning, provide details on how you will integrate these considerations into the lesson plan.
6. Supporting Materials: If implementation of the lesson will require supporting materials, list them here. Supporting materials might include emotion charts, graphic organizers, fidgets, Power Cards,* etc.	

Name: ______________________
Date: ______________________
Class/Teacher: ______________________
Unit: ______________________

Lesson Plan a la Carte
SOLO Planning Step 2

SOLO Lesson Plan

**Each staff in the classroom receives a double-sided copy of this plan.*

INTEGRATED LESSON PLAN		**Date of Implementation:**	
1. Name & Brief Description of the Lesson:			
2. Learning Objective(s):			
3. Implementation			
Activity	**Strategies for Implementation**	**Supporting Materials**	**Lead**

5. ASSESSMENT **Date:**

Rate the Lesson
On a scale of 1 to 5, rate how you feel the lesson generally went.

1	2	3	4	5
poorly		okay		very well

Notes:

Learning Objectives
Were the Learning Objectives satisfied?
☐ no ☐ partially ☐ yes
Notes:

Considerations for Planning
Were the Considerations for Planning successfully considered or implemented?
☐ no ☐ partially ☐ yes
Notes:

Name: ______________________
Date: ______________________
Class/Teacher: ______________________
Unit: ______________________

Lesson Plan a la Carte
SOLO Planning Step 2

SOLO Lesson Plan Cont.

Implementation Cont.			
Activity	**Strategies for Implementation**	**Supporting Materials**	**Lead & Team Supports**

4. School Documentation & Protocols

ASSESSMENT Cont.

Staff Roles
Were staff roles during implementation clear & successfully executed?
☐ no ☐ partially ☐ yes
Notes:

Obstacles to Learning
Revisit the obstacles to learning that you identified in your draft. Were the obstacles addressed by the lesson plan?
☐ no ☐ partially ☐ yes
Notes:

Documentation
Will you use this lesson plan as evidence for documenting IEP fidelity, IEP goals, SDI, RTI or other mandates/protocols? ☐ no ☐ yes
Notes:

P.O. Box 23173
Overland Park, Kansas 66283-0173
www.aapcpublishing.net